HOW TO
WRITE
A NOVEL

FROM IDEA TO BOOK

Joanna Penn

How to Write a Novel: From Idea to Book

Copyright © Joanna Penn (2022)

All rights reserved. No part of this publication may be reproduced, stored in a retrieval system, or transmitted, in any form or by any means, without the prior written permission of the publisher.

Paperback ISBN: 978-1-915425-09-6
Large Print ISBN: 978-1-915425-12-6
Hardback ISBN: 978-1-915425-13-3
Ebook ISBN: 978-1-915425-08-9
Audiobook ISBN: 978-1-915425-10-2
Workbook ISBN: 978-1-915425-11-9

Published by Curl Up Press

Requests to publish work from this book should be sent to: joanna@TheCreativePenn.com

Cover and Interior Design: JD Smith

www.CurlUpPress.com

"Measure your life
by what
you create."

Joanna Penn

Contents

Introduction   1

Part 1: First Principles   9

    1.1   Why are you writing a novel?   11
    1.2   What has stopped you from completing a novel before?   17
    1.3   Principles to keep in mind as you create   25

Part 2: Ideas, Research, Plotting, and Discovery Writing   37

    2.1   How to find and capture ideas   39
    2.2   How to research your novel and when to stop   58
    2.3   Outlining (or plotting)   69
    2.4   Discovery writing (or pantsing)   78
    2.5   What are you writing? Genre   92
    2.6   What are you writing? Short story, novella, or novel   104
    2.7   What are you writing? Stand-alone, series, or serial   107

Part 3: Aspects of a Novel — 115

   3.1 Story structure — 117
   3.2 Scenes and chapters — 128
   3.3 Character: Who is the story about? — 138
   3.4 Point of view — 165
   3.5 Dialogue — 175
   3.6 Plot: What happens in the story? — 186
   3.7 Conflict — 205
   3.8 Openings and endings — 210
   3.9 Setting and world-building: Where does the story happen? — 217
   3.10 Author voice — 231
   3.11 Theme — 235
   3.12 Book or story title — 242
   3.13 Language versus story and tools versus art — 248

Part 4: Writing the First Draft — 251

   4.1 Attitude to the first draft — 253
   4.2 How to write the first draft — 260
   4.3 Dictate your book — 274
   4.4 Write fast, cycle through, or write slow — 284
   4.5 Writer's block — 290
   4.6 Writing tools and software — 298
   4.7 When is the first draft finished? — 305

Part 5: The Editing Process — 311

- 5.1 Overview of the editing process — 313
- 5.2 Self-editing — 319
- 5.3 How to find and work with a professional editor — 334
- 5.4 Beta readers, specialist readers, and sensitivity readers — 346
- 5.5 Editing tools and software — 352
- 5.6 Lessons learned from editing my first novel after more than a decade — 356
- 5.7 When is the book finished? — 377

Conclusion — 381
Need more help? — 388
More Books And Courses From Joanna Penn — 389
About Joanna Penn — 393
Appendix 1: Bibliography — 395
Appendix 2: List of Questions — 404
Acknowledgments — 427

Introduction

Writing a novel will change your life.

It might not be in the way that you expect, but when you hold your book in your hand and say, "I made this," something will shift. The process of getting to that point will light a spark in your creative soul and help you discover unexpected aspects of yourself. It will be one of the things you are most proud of in your life. It will be worth the effort.

My goal with this book is to help you get there.

But *How to Write a Novel* is not an exhaustive tome of everything you could ever learn about writing. I have deliberately cut it down as much as possible.

The writing craft is like an iceberg.

You can write a novel with the basic knowledge that you can see above the surface. The hidden depths of the writing craft, like the iceberg, go much deeper than you can imagine. Learning it all cannot be achieved in a single lifetime, and that is part of the joy of being a writer. You learn something new with every story you write and every book that emerges into the world.

But you don't need to know it all in order to get started.

In fact, if you wait until you know everything about the writing craft before you start your novel, you will be overwhelmed with too much information and, most likely, never finish.

This book will help those writing their first novel and also those who want to revisit the creative process. It covers the basic knowledge above the surface of the iceberg and hints at the depths beneath.

What sets this book apart is that I'm an intuitive discovery writer. I don't plot or outline. Most craft books are written by plotters, outliners, and linear thinkers, so hopefully, I can also provide a different perspective.

You can certainly write and finish a novel with the information in this book, but there's always more to learn. The writing craft is the journey of a lifetime. Let's take the first step together.

You can learn how to write a novel

I used to think that authors sat at their desks, and perfect words flowed effortlessly from their fingertips. I thought that the sentences in the pages of a finished book emerged from the author's mind fully formed. That writers entered a state of flow and wrote without effort. In fact, if it was difficult, and they struggled, perhaps they weren't a 'real' writer at all. Perhaps they didn't have talent or a gift for writing and, of course, that meant I could never write a novel because I, too, had neither.

But that is not the reality of the writing life.

The words you read in a finished novel result from hard work, occasional moments of flow and flashes of insight, and an editorial process that transforms the first draft into a finished book.

Too many new writers give up because they don't know the next step to take, or they find that writing a novel is harder than they expect. But it's worth the effort, I promise you, and this book will help you through the journey.

Who am I?

Like you, I'm a reader and I love books. I read every day — for escape, fun, and solace, as well as for entertainment, education, and inspiration. I spend way too much money on books!

When I was a little girl, I would toddle into my mum's bedroom at night. Instead of a teddy, I would drag my favorite books in with me and curl up at the end of the bed with them in my arms.

I remember little about what happened at school or even university, but I remember so many of the books I read along the way. The written word has always been my happy place. Perhaps that's also true for you.

I never thought I could be a fiction writer. Such a rarefied breed of miraculous creatures surely lived in ivory towers somewhere inaccessible to mere mortals. Those who could turn their thoughts into words were so far away from my experience, there was no way I could ever talk to them, let alone become one.

But if writing is the way you express yourself, if writing is the way you figure out the world, if writing is your art and your joy and the thing you do that makes life make sense — then you must write.

Eventually, I discovered this truth and gave myself permission to write more than just my journals.

I started writing nonfiction for publication in 2006 and wrote the first five thousand words of my first novel in 2009.

Since then, I've written eighteen novels and novellas, in addition to many short stories, as J.F. Penn, and co-written several others. I'm an award-nominated, *New York Times* and *USA Today* bestseller, and I've sold nearly a million books in over one hundred countries and multiple languages.

I certainly don't know everything about the writing craft, but I hope my insights from the author journey will be useful for you.

How to read the book

It's been a challenge to structure the material in this book because, for me, writing a novel is about wrangling chaos. I've never had a linear process — either for learning how to write, or for crafting my own novels.

Some authors are structured and organized, and others are more intuitive. But most writers do not progress from story idea to characters to plot to theme in an organized fashion every time. Most do not write the first line of the first paragraph and then proceed all the way to The End in order.

Creation is not a linear process.

It's more like a whirlwind — at least it is for me. A tornado of ideas and characters and plot points and deeper themes and images and so much more, all whirling around in no particular order.

My job as an author is to wrangle that chaos. To capture the whirlwind and channel it into a linear story for the reader to experience, while still retaining the kinetic energy of the original spark.

When you're starting out, the chaos can seem overwhelming, but when you've written a few books, you discover the wrangling process is part of the joy of creation.

I have wrangled the material of this book in the same way. You can read in order or jump to a particular section depending on how you prefer to learn.

Part 1 covers mindset issues, helping you better understand why you want to write, what may have stopped you in the past, and the five principles that will help you make progress now.

Part 2 delves into how to generate ideas, conduct

research, and find a writing process that works for you—whether you are an outliner or a discovery writer, or something in between.

Part 3 guides you through the major aspects of the craft of writing a novel, from story structure to author voice.

Part 4 will help you start and finish your first draft, including tips on both mindset and writing tools.

Part 5 focuses on the editing process, with advice on self-editing and working with a professional editor.

There are lots of tips and ideas and processes that might help — but please discard those that don't work for you. Ultimately, there are no rules, only suggestions from authors who have written the path before you.

We all have to find our own way through wrangling the chaos to a finished novel. You *will* find your own path, but you might take a few wrong turns and go down some blind alleys before you make it to the finish line.

There are questions at the end of every chapter that might help. You might know the answers right away, you might discover them later, or you might never know — and that's okay, too.

Writing a novel will change your life — so let's get started.

* * *

You can download the questions, bibliography, and more resources at:

www.TheCreativePenn.com/writenoveldownload

If you'd like to work through the material in writing, you can find the print edition of *How to Write a Novel: Companion Workbook* at:

www.TheCreativePenn.com/writenovelworkbook

* * *

Note: There are affiliate links within this book to products and services that I recommend and use personally. If you buy through my link, I receive a small percentage of the sale at no extra cost to you, and in some cases, you may receive a discount. I only recommend products and services that I believe are great for writers, so I hope you find them useful.

Part 1: First Principles

1.1 Why are you writing a novel?

> "The novel, I submit, is an unparalleled vehicle for self-discovery."
>
> —*Lawrence Block,*
> *Writing the Novel From Plot to Print to Pixel*

Take a deep breath and be really honest with yourself.

Why do you want to write this novel?

If you've never written one before, why do you want to put yourself through the process? What's driving you forward?

If you've already written other novels, why are you writing this particular book?

It's not easy to write a novel. Many people say they want to write one, but few of them finish a first draft. Even fewer will hold their finished book in their hands, and even fewer will find success, however they define it.

There's a lot to learn and you will have to overcome challenges, both practical and emotional, to finish your book, so you need a driving reason to see you through the difficult times ahead.

Here are some possible reasons:

- There's a story burning in my heart that I have to tell
- This character keeps nudging me or talking to me and I need to get them out of my head
- I've always been a reader, and now I want to be a writer
- I have this inner need to write something
- I love reading but I can't find the book I really want to read, so I might as well write it myself
- I want validation that I can write something good
- It's one of my life goals — I've always wanted to write a book and now I'm determined to achieve it
- I want to win a literary prize
- I want to change the world, and stories are the best way to shift people's mindset
- I want to make money with my stories, hopefully, lots of money!

- Writing my story as fiction will help me heal, and hopefully help others too
- I want to see my story on the screen as a film or a TV show
- I have so many ideas and I need to turn those into books

Whatever your reasons, identify them now. You might need to dig down a layer or two because sometimes our desires go deeper than we think.

> "Writing isn't about making money, getting famous, getting dates, getting laid, or making friends. In the end, it's about enriching the lives of those who will read your work, and enriching your own life, as well."
>
> —*Stephen King, On Writing*

Why do I write fiction?

I started my first novel as a writing challenge. A guest on my podcast, Tom Evans, suggested that I might have a block about writing a novel, even though I had already written several nonfiction books. I put fiction writing on a pedestal and couldn't see myself as creative enough to write stories, yet I also yearned to be a 'real' writer. Tom suggested I give fiction writing a go.

So, I joined NaNoWriMo, National Novel Writing Month, in November 2009. I wrote around 20,000 words and discovered a spark of an idea. That spark encouraged me — perhaps I could write a novel after all. I lived in Brisbane, Australia, at the time and I enrolled in The Year of the Novel at the Queensland State Library and spent the next fourteen months writing and editing.

I loved the writing process, and I found myself overflowing with ideas for other stories. I caught the writing bug big time!

Now I write for a different reason.

I measure my life by what I create.

I enjoy (almost) every part of the creative process. Of course, there are challenges and days where writing feels like a slog, but the effort makes it even more worthwhile. I love holding a finished book in my hand and saying, "I made this!"

I also have an audience of readers waiting for the story. Writing is my passion, but it's also my job. I'm a full-time author, so my books also bring me income, now and into the future. But at heart, it's still about the creative process and what I discover along the way about the story — and about myself.

Your reasons for writing will change over time, but identifying them can sustain you through the journey, wherever you are right now.

> "The writing process alchemically alters me, leaving me transformed."
>
> —bell hooks, *Remembered Rapture*

Questions:

- Why do you want to write a novel?
- Go deeper. What are the reasons behind that?
- Are these reasons enough to carry you through difficult times?

Resources:

- *On Writing: A Memoir of the Craft* — Stephen King
- *Remembered Rapture: The Writer at Work* — bell hooks
- *Writing the Novel From Plot to Print to Pixel* — Lawrence Block
- Episode 500 of The Creative Penn Podcast where I replay Tom's comments and discuss how they shaped my creative direction — www.TheCreativePenn.com/500

1.2 What has stopped you from completing a novel before?

How long have you been thinking about writing a novel?

For many writers, it's been years, perhaps even as long as they can remember.

Why haven't you written your novel yet? Or, if you started once, why didn't you finish?

What stopped you before — and how can you break through that barrier now?

Here are some common reasons writers quit:

- I'm overwhelmed with too much information. It's too complicated.
- I don't know enough. I don't know where to start.
- I don't have enough time. There are always more important things to do.
- I'm worried that I might not be good enough. What if my writing is terrible?

- What if I fail? I'm going to look really stupid and I'll be embarrassed.
- It might be a waste of time.
- I don't have any ideas.
- I have too many ideas.
- I want to write something but I don't know what.
- I got lost in the plot, and couldn't turn my thoughts into words.
- I have a terrible draft, but I don't know how to finish.
- Someone told me my writing was terrible (a teacher, an editor, a friend, a loved one) and I can't get past that.
- I keep starting and then running out of steam, so I never finish.

Whatever you're feeling, you're the only one who can work through the obstacles and shift your mindset.

You have to want to write your novel. You have to be determined to finish it.

It's time to overcome those issues and make it happen.

The rest of this book will help with the practical side, but let's tackle some of the possible barriers right now.

"I don't have the time."

The COVID-19 pandemic changed so much for so many and reminded us all that life is short.

Memento mori. Remember, you will die.

If you don't write your novel, will you regret it?

If yes, then make the time.

> "There are years that ask the question and years that answer."
>
> —Zora Neale Hurston,
> *Their Eyes Were Watching God*

Self-doubt and 'comparisonitis'

Self-doubt is part of the creative process. Most of us think our writing is terrible at some point, and most of us compare ourselves to successful writers and find ourselves wanting.

In my early years of fiction writing, I attended ThrillerFest in New York and listened to a panel with some of the biggest names in the thriller genre. Lee

Child, of Jack Reacher fame; David Morrell, who wrote *First Blood*, which became *Rambo*; action-adventure writer Clive Cussler; R.L. Stine, who has sold over 400 million books; romantic suspense mega-bestseller Sandra Brown; and others. All of them career authors with decades of experience, and all multi-*New York Times* bestsellers.

Someone in the audience stood up and said, "I feel like my story is no good. How can I get over that?"

All the writers on the panel nodded and said a variation of, "Every time I write something, I think it's a pile of crap. Every time I put a book out, I wonder whether this time they'll find out that I am some kind of fraud."

All writers experience the cycle of self-doubt, but the successful ones learn to live with it. Career authors understand it's part of the creative process and don't let it get in the way of writing and finishing their books.

> "Bad writers tend to have self-confidence while the good ones tend to have self-doubt."
>
> —*Charles Bukowski*

Fear of failure

Fear comes from that ancient part of the brain that protects us from lions and bears and physical violence, but also from the things that might harm us psychologically. If we avoid them all, we will never be hurt.

Fear around writing can feel just as serious as any other kind of fear, but you have to decide whether it's worth facing.

What is failure for you?

Not finishing the book? Not getting an agent or a publisher? Self-publishing and not selling anything? Getting bad reviews?

You don't have to face any of these if you don't write. Only you can make that choice.

> "The life creative is never—ever—lived without frightening, intoxicating risk."
>
> —David duChemin, *A Beautiful Anarchy*

Fear of judgment

What will people think of me if I write this?

Will they hate me? Or think I'm weird, or disturbed? Will they cast me out and say horrible things about me? Will I get reviews that break my heart?

This is definitely something that comes up for me, and it results in self-censorship because you will struggle to write what you really want to write.

It took me four novels to stop self-censoring. *Desecration* was my fifth novel, and it's the one that reveals a side of me I had kept hidden until then. It released me.

Sometimes it takes time to chip away at the layers we protect ourselves with.

But that's okay.

The writing process works its magic — word after word, day after day.

How can you tackle these fears?

You can prevent the fear of writing something terrible from becoming a reality by improving your craft and using a rigorous editorial process, as I'll explain later. But you also need to accept that fear is part of the creative journey. If you don't feel it, perhaps you're not writing what's truly on your heart.

You can also write under another name if that helps. I love writing fiction under J.F. Penn, although it is hardly a pseudonym. It's pretty obvious that it's me, but it separates my self-help, upbeat, positive side from my darker, more contemplative novelist persona. Using a different name might help you manage the fear of judgment; it's a common approach adopted by many authors.

You can find more help in my book, *The Successful Author Mindset: A Handbook for Surviving the Writer's Journey*.

> "Do you have the courage to bring forth the treasures that are in you?"
>
> —Elizabeth Gilbert, *Big Magic*

Questions:

- How long have you been thinking about writing a novel?
- Why haven't you written your novel before? Or, if you started, why didn't you finish? What stopped you — and how can you break through that barrier now?
- Are you going to finish the novel this time?

Resources:

- *A Beautiful Anarchy: When The Life Creative Becomes The Life Created* — David duChemin
- *Big Magic: Creative Living Beyond Fear* — Elizabeth Gilbert
- *The Successful Author Mindset: A Handbook for Surviving the Writer's Journey* — Joanna Penn

1.3 Principles to keep in mind as you create

In future chapters, we'll explore the details of writing a novel, but first I want to walk you through five key principles I've learned in over a decade of being a full-time writer.

(1) Create in a way that works for your personality and lifestyle

I'm sure you've read many writing craft books. They all have great suggestions, but although you can pick up tips in all of them — including this one — it's unlikely that you will write your novel in exactly the same way as anyone else.

It's taken me more than a decade to embrace being an intuitive discovery writer. I have tried over and over again to outline and become more analytical in my process because that's what 'everyone' says is the best way.

But every time I tried, I felt miserable because it was so hard and didn't feel creative to me. I needed to find my own process to wrangle the chaos.

I've looked at authors who write a book a month

with envy, and recommitted myself to spending more hours in the chair to be more like them.

But that made me miserable too.

I love writing fiction, but it's not the only thing for me. I am a multi-passionate creative. I love writing nonfiction; I love podcasting and creating audio; I love researching futurist things; I love experimenting. I love traveling and (sometimes) speaking on different topics. I do not want to spend my whole working life in the fiction chair.

I've tried to write to market. I've tried to focus on one series. I've tried co-writing fiction. None of these things resonate with my creative soul.

You must find what's right for your personality and your lifestyle.

Are you an outliner or a discovery writer?

Are you a morning person or a night owl?

Do you love the routine of creating every day no matter what, or do you prefer binge writing?

Do you write messy first drafts or perfect every sentence from the beginning?

Part of the process of writing a novel is getting to know yourself and reflecting honestly about how things work for you as you try them out.

Of course, you have to give things a go in order to know whether they might work, but then tune into your feelings. Does it feel right for you? What other options could you try?

You might also find various personality tests useful. There are lots of them, but personally, I found the Myers-Briggs insightful because I didn't know I was an introvert until my thirties. I just thought I was weird and didn't really fit well into society. Once I discovered that I'm an INFJ, everything made sense!

I also found the CliftonStrengths Assessment useful. Becca Syme's books explore how these strengths work for writers, in particular.

> You can listen to or read an interview with Becca at:

www.TheCreativePenn.com/strengths

(2) Identify the books you love — not the ones you've been told to appreciate

I studied English literature at school and read the classics. I was educated to think that the only books worth reading were those that won prizes of some kind, and the only books worth writing were literary fiction.

But the books I loved as a teenager were the Hardy Boys' adventures and Wilbur Smith's African stories. I wanted to watch *The A-Team* at the weekend with all its explosive fun, and I always loved James Bond movies.

Many years later, when I worked as an IT consultant implementing accounts payable systems, I would read thrillers on the commuter train to work. I'd go to the bookshop at lunchtimes to buy more stories. Anything to escape the day job I hated and a life I didn't know how I'd ended up living.

When *The Da Vinci Code* by Dan Brown hit the bestseller charts, I saw the possibilities for writing fiction that would both interest me in the research process and also satisfy my love of thrillers.

I enjoy an introspective literary story now and then,

but mostly, I want to escape into action adventure with monsters, good conquering evil, and conspiracies — everything that is *not* my life.

As a reader, I only read books I love.

As an author, I only write the books I love and want to read.

Identify the books you really love, not the ones that other people tell you are somehow more worthy than others.

Write a list of five to ten books you love and keep adding to it as you think of more. This will help in writing your novel, so be honest. No one needs to see it.

(3) Don't overcomplicate the writing process

I spent many years reading books on the craft and doing courses before I wrote anything myself. But my writing life changed when I attended a workshop at the Sydney Writers' Festival back when I lived in Australia.

I entered the workshop ready to listen, learn, and take notes. I'm a total geek and I like taking notes. It feels constructive and there are words on the page by the end of the session, even if they are not my own thoughts.

But the instructor didn't start teaching.

He said, "Let's start with a writing exercise."

I sat there, my hand frozen over my notebook. *What? You mean I actually have to make something up?!*

He said, "Write about when you discovered something for real that you already knew in your heart to be true. You have ten minutes."

He clicked a button on a timer.

There was quiet in the room — the scratching of pens on paper the only sound.

As the other students began writing, I didn't want to look like I didn't know what I was doing. So I started writing — and the words came.

That first timed session changed my life. It forced me to write my own words rather than taking notes on yet more information. It kicked me out of learning brain, and into a creative state where I produced my own work.

It doesn't matter what I wrote that day, and I can't remember anything else from that session. But my original words made sense on the page. They needed editing, for sure, but it was a start.

That first timed writing block made it possible for me to imagine doing it again, and again, and again.

That's basically what you have to do to write a novel.

Write words from your mind onto a page repeatedly. You have to make the time for it, and then you have to show up and write the words.

Again and again and again.

Of course, there are many more aspects to the writing craft, but at heart, this is the action that will enable you to complete a novel.

If you already have a creative writing practice, this

might be old news. But if you have never done a timed writing session before, then start now.

Open a blank page in your notebook or a new window on whatever device you write on.

Find a writing prompt, or just start with "I remember…"

Set a timer for ten minutes.

Write.

> "Don't wait until you know who you are to get started. It's in the act of making things and doing our work that we figure out who we are."
>
> —Austin Kleon, *Steal Like An Artist*

(4) Keep your story simple

We've all spent a lifetime exploring worlds through books, films, audio, games, and life experience. When it comes to writing a novel, all those influences emerge and we can quickly become bogged down.

So many characters, so many plot possibilities, so many emotional dramas, so much everything… then we add to the mix all the writing craft books and workshops and podcasts and all the knowledge we've picked up along the way and want to incorporate.

It compounds into something gigantic that is so daunting we don't even start, or we start and then fail at the first hurdle because it's just too difficult.

So keep it simple. All you need for a story is:

- A character
- In a setting
- Who has a goal
- Who has to overcome all kinds of conflict on the way to achieving that goal while
- Someone or something tries to stop them along the way

- The character either achieves their goal or fails
- And along the way, they go through some kind of transformation

If you find yourself lost in too much detail at any point, return to this roadmap. Stop and simplify.

(5) Be patient — remember your writing age

Whatever your actual age, you also have a writing age.

This is true of anything you want to master. You need practice to improve.

Compare a martial artist in their first year to someone with twenty years' experience. Or a painter, a business executive, a yoga practitioner.

Regardless of the profession or hobby, someone in year twenty will be better than someone in year one. If it's a job, they will also be paid more because of their expertise.

The same is true with writing.

No one exits the womb knowing how to write a novel. You have to learn. Don't compare yourself to someone whose writing age is greater than yours.

I love many of Stephen King's books, and it's daunting to compare my writing to his masterpieces. But he is almost thirty years older than me, and he started writing in his teens. At the time of writing, King's fiction-writing age is around sixty, whereas my fiction-writing age is eleven. How can I compare myself to somebody who has had that much practice? It's like someone who's done a couple of violin lessons comparing themselves to the greatest violin player at Carnegie Hall.

Be patient and keep writing, keep reading, keep practicing. After all, you're a writer. What else would you rather be doing?!

Questions:

- What do you already know about your personality and your lifestyle that might impact your writing craft?
- Have you tried different personality tests? If you haven't, how might they help you?
- How can you remain aware of what creative practices work for you along the way?
- What are the books (and films) that you truly love, rather than the ones you have been told

to value by others? Write your list of five to ten.

- Do you already have a timed writing practice? If not, do it now. Open a blank page. Find a writing prompt, or just start with "I remember…" Set a timer for ten minutes. Write.
- If you feel resistance to this practice, identify why and how you might overcome it.
- How can you keep your story simple?
- What is your writing age? What is the writing age of the author whose work you love the most?

Resources:

- *Steal Like An Artist: 10 Things Nobody Told You About Being Creative* — Austin Kleon
- *The Creative Habit: Learn It and Use It for Life* — Twyla Tharp
- *Writing Down the Bones: Freeing the Writer Within*
  — Natalie Goldberg
- Strengths for Writers. Interview with Becca Syme
  — www.TheCreativePenn.com/strengths

Part 2: Ideas, Research, Plotting, and Discovery Writing

2.1 How to find and capture ideas

When authors are interviewed, one question comes up over and over again: "Where do you get your ideas?"

Once you have trained the idea muscle, ideas are abundant — you will have thousands of them. The problem is deciding which to pay attention to since you don't have the time to turn all of them into stories.

But I still remember when I started out as a writer and this question was one I fixated on, too.

At the time, I wrote technical specifications for programmers in my IT consulting day job. I didn't feel creative at all. I couldn't understand where story ideas came from. It seemed as if they happened by magic to other people, but remained out of my reach.

It took time to retrain my mind and open myself up to creativity and ideas. But eventually, they started to flow.

Here are some tips if this is something you struggle with, too.

Recognize your curiosity and lean into it

What catches your attention?

If you're in a bookstore, which area do you visit? What covers catch your eye? What do you like to read about?

If you're in a new city, how do you spend your time? If you're sitting in a cafe, why do you notice some people more than others?

What films or TV shows or documentaries do you watch? What do you take photos of?

What catches your eye and stops you scrolling on social media?

What do you listen to on podcasts or the radio?

We're surrounded by an overwhelming amount of stimuli — sights and sounds and smells and things happening around us all the time. We can't take it all in. We have to tune in to specific aspects of the world. We experience life with a filter based on our interests. The trick is to pay more attention to that filter, widening it, leaning into it, or shifting it to find ideas.

I love visiting historical places with religious significance. I love art and architecture with deep cultural meaning; as I explore, I tune into my curiosity and notice questions and ideas as they come, jotting them down in a journal or in my phone.

As an example, we visited Amsterdam for a long weekend one spring. Along with a canal boat trip and a walk in the tulip fields, we also visited the Portuguese Synagogue. It's a beautiful building with the oldest functioning Jewish library in the world, but it also sparked my curiosity.

Why is there a Portuguese Synagogue in the heart of Amsterdam (which is in the Netherlands, not Portugal)?

What manuscripts might be within the mysterious library?

While browsing the synagogue shop, I picked up a curious nonfiction book, *Jewish Pirates of the Caribbean: How a Generation of Swashbuckling Jews Carved Out an Empire in the New World in Their Quest for Treasure, Religious Freedom—and Revenge* by Edward Kritzler. I had to buy it! The ideas sparked by that one visit turned into *Tree of Life*, a modern-day thriller based on the history of the Portuguese empire.

If you can't identify what you're curious about right away, don't worry. It takes practice to recognize it and allow it to emerge, especially if you've spent years as an adult pursuing more 'appropriate' interests.

We learn to repress our curiosity as we grow up, so think back before real life stopped you doing things for the fun of it.

What were you curious about when you were younger?

What do you like helping your kids or grandkids or other children in your life with?

What are the standout memories of your life?

What topics won't let you go?

Idea generation is like a muscle. When you visit a gym for the first time, you have to start with tiny weights. Over time, you work up to heavier ones.

Start small by noticing what you're interested in and lean into those preferences. You will find the practice compounds until, one day, you'll be struggling with the number of ideas you have!

Go on an Artist's Date

If you try to create from an empty mind, you will find yourself blocked pretty fast because there's nothing for your imagination to work with. You need to fill your creative well in order to write.

The idea of the Artist's Date comes from Julia Cameron's *The Artist's Way* and it's a staple of my creative practice. I need to consume in order to produce.

Book time out for your creative self and go somewhere that will open your mind and challenge you in a new way. An art gallery, a museum, a seminar, or just time away from the usual routine to read a book or watch a film or whatever your inner artist wants to do.

Go alone so you can tune into your thoughts and preferences rather than what others think. Notice how you feel and consider questions that arise.

I will never forget the visceral feeling in my gut when I walked into the Hunterian Museum at the Royal College of Surgeons in London for the first time. The walls of specimen jars filled with grotesque body parts sparked the idea for my crime thriller *Desecration*, and now I love visiting anatomy museums when I travel.

Take a notebook on your Artist's Date and spend time writing. Little notes and impressions, thoughts, and feelings are fine at this stage. You don't need to produce anything coherent. You're just filling the well and seeing how it goes. Resist the urge to check email or social media or take yourself out of the experience while you are in it.

When you're finished, schedule the next one.

> "The most creative people I know fill their brains, their idea factories, with as much raw material as they can… The more we increase our inputs, the more we increase possibilities."
>
> —David duChemin, *A Beautiful Anarchy*

Notice what fascinates you about people

You need characters for your stories, so start to consider what fascinates you about people.

What job do they have? Why do they do it? What choices have they made? What are their interesting hobbies? How do they speak? What's their family like? How does their experience impact their life now?

Sometimes a character alone will inspire an idea. My short story, *Blood, Sweat, and Flame,* was inspired by the Netflix series *Blown Away*. It's set in a glassblowing hotshop and explores how far a glass artist might go to win critical acclaim for their work.

But sometimes, it's just about a vague idea that something might be interesting. I'm reading about war photographers and journalists at the moment, those professionals who choose to put themselves in physical danger for a story. What drives them to go back even after a near death experience? I've read novels, memoirs, and nonfiction about war photographers, but as I write this, I don't have a story for the emerging character. I'm just filling the creative well and I trust that the story will arrive at some point. Maybe even by the time you read this.

Notice interesting objects and artifacts

In thrillers, action adventure, and some mysteries, there is often a particular object that the characters search for — nicknamed the MacGuffin — and it's intriguing enough to become the center of the story. The Holy Grail and the Ark of the Covenant are two MacGuffins that endure in stories through countless re-tellings.

I use MacGuffins in my ARKANE thrillers and they often inspire a story. On a trip to Budapest, we visited the Basilica to see the thousand-year-old mummified hand of Saint István. Not many countries have a mummified hand at the heart of their most famous cathedral! As I stood there gazing at it, I wondered what would happen if someone stole this important religious and national symbol? Who would do such a thing and why?

When we visited Dohány Street Synagogue later that weekend, and learned what happened to the Jews of the area, I considered how history might repeat itself and that became the seed of *One Day in Budapest*.

Use real events and places to spark ideas

Best friends Ben and Lucy are sailing on the ocean beyond Christchurch, New Zealand. They look to the horizon and see a huge tidal wave bearing down on them…

This scene opens *Risen Gods*, my dark fantasy novel co-written with J. Thorn, inspired by the real events of the 2011 Christchurch earthquake.

New Zealand is on the Pacific Rim of Fire and has

a lot of volcanic activity. I lived there for several years and I'm a New Zealand citizen, so I know the country well.

I wondered what would happen if you lived through one of these natural disasters, then considered a dark fantasy spin on the idea. What if the gods of New Zealand decided to take their land back from the humans who abused it so much?

Don't worry if a historical event has been used before as new research emerges all the time, and your story will always have your take on the topic.

There are countless novels based on Nazi Germany. All have the same underlying aspect of the horrors of the Holocaust, but the books end up completely different. Compare *Schindler's Ark*, *Sophie's Choice*, and *The Man in the High Castle*.

Consider 'What if?' ideas

"What if" questions are often the basis for books.

The Martian by Andy Weir: What if you were stuck alone on Mars?

Fifty Shades of Grey by E.L. James: What if you met a sexy billionaire who offered you everything you ever wanted in exchange for something unexpected in the bedroom?

The Stand by Stephen King: What if a plague wiped out 99 percent of the population and you were one of the few left?

Consider the 'what if' questions behind the books you love; you could answer the same question in a different way in your own story.

Use quotes to spark ideas

The title of my thriller *Destroyer of Worlds* comes from the quote, "I am become death, destroyer of worlds."

It's originally from the Bhagavad Gita, but was also quoted by Oppenheimer after the test of the first atomic bomb. It simultaneously encapsulates ideas about Hindu gods and nuclear weapons and sparked a question in my mind. How could a Hindu artifact destroy the world?

I cover research in more detail in the next chapter, but if you write down a quote to use later, put it in quotation marks and attribute it in case you want to use it later.

Tap into themes and issues you care about — but don't preach

Many authors base their stories on important societal issues and themes that they have a personal connection to.

The Handmaid's Tale by Margaret Atwood was published in 1985, and I studied it as part of my English literature course in the early '90s. Its theme of feminism and women's rights was important back then, but the book was given a new lease of life during the #MeToo era and adapted for a popular TV series. In 2022, the Roe versus Wade ruling on abortion in the USA became a flash point for controversy fifty years after it was first passed. The theme of women's rights made headlines once more, and of course, has sparked additional important stories.

Different societal issues drive authors to write, depending on their worldview. Is there an issue or cause you feel passionately about? You must decide what's important enough for you to write a story about, or if you want to keep your stories for entertainment or escape.

Whatever cause you are passionate about, you're writing a story, not a nonfiction book on the topic or an essay preaching your point of view. Don't bash the reader over the head with your stance. Tell a story and use your theme to underpin the characters and the plot.

But remember, you do not have to write an important story. You can just write for fun. Readers need that, too. Perhaps now more than ever.

> "You are not required to save the world with your creativity. Your art not only doesn't need to be original… it also doesn't have to be *important*."
>
> —Elizabeth Gilbert, Big Magic

Use ideas from other books, stories, and myths

My short story collection, *A Thousand Fiendish Angels*, is based on Dante's *Inferno*. The digital retailer Kobo commissioned the stories for the launch of Dan Brown's thriller *Inferno* in 2014.

Dante's *Inferno* is out of copyright, so you can do whatever you like with it. I made notes on the book and copied out lines I liked, words that resonated, and character ideas. For example, in my story, the Minotaur becomes a depraved ruler of the post-apocalyptic city of Dis.

Many writers use the classics for inspiration. For example, Madeline Miller has written fictional accounts of Circe, Achilles, and other characters from Greek myth. *The Hunger Games* by Suzanne Collins was inspired by the myth of Theseus and the Minotaur, in which tributes were offered to the monster every year.

If you take notes from other books, don't copy out entire passages word-for-word because you may end up accidentally plagiarizing. But certainly you can get ideas from other books, then spin off and write your own version.

Mine your own depths

Joseph Campbell said, "It is by going down into the abyss that we recover the treasures of life." Oprah Winfrey said, "Turn your wounds into wisdom."

Your experience and life history, your relationships, your fears and joys can all find their way into your stories.

Your questions can, too.

My ARKANE thrillers are underpinned by the question of whether God exists and what lies beyond this physical realm. I'm not religious, but I am a seeker and I have had spiritual experiences at different places and at different times that I weave into my stories.

You will find gold in your own deeper side that you can excavate for your creative journey.

* * *

So now you have a myriad of ideas, what do you do with them?

Capture your ideas somehow

Whether you outline or you're a discovery writer, you will end up with all kinds of notes and ideas and photos and scraps of paper and computer files, as well as website links, books, and other inspirational odds and ends. You need a way to keep track of everything, as you cannot keep it all in your head.

Some authors don't write their ideas down, trusting they will re-emerge if they are important enough. But most find a method of recording them somehow.

I use the Things app on my phone to capture ideas on the go. I use journals for research trips and taking notes on books. (Leuchtturm or Moleskine, A5, plain paper, with covers in teal, turquoise, or scarlet, if you're a journal geek like me!)

I use Scrivener to gather notes together once I'm further into a project. Others use programs such as Evernote or Notion. Some use index cards or physical boxes and folders.

There are no rules. Do whatever works for you.

I find myself browsing through these idea archives sometimes, digging out old ideas and combining them with new ones for stories. It's always interesting to revisit my past self and wonder what I was thinking at the time.

What if someone steals my idea?

This is a common worry for new authors, but the truth is that ideas are so abundant as to be worthless. When you fix an idea into words, it transforms into something separate from the idea itself. The same idea will turn into different stories when written by a different author. Execution is everything.

You might have an amazing idea, but it will float away into the ether unless you turn it into a book readers might love. That said, there will always be more ideas, so don't obsess about a particular one. Keep filling the creative well, keep writing, and more will come.

What if my idea has been written before?

There will always be universal story elements and emotions that resonate with readers. Consider *Romeo and Juliet* and *Titanic*. No one would say these two are the same, and yet, at heart, they are classic love stories featuring characters from different worlds with a tragic ending.

Originality and creativity come from combining multiple influences into something new, and adding your experience into the expression of an idea so it becomes something fresh.

How do I choose which idea to work on?

Once you tune into your curiosity, you will come up against the 'problem' of having too many ideas.

I have hundreds of notes in my ideas folder, but some keep coming back. Those that nudge at my mind are the ones I investigate further. Some are scraps that might turn into a short story, and others are seed ideas that could span a whole series.

Usually something happens to push me in a specific direction. I do a research trip that helps me settle on one idea over another, or I just have an intuitive sense of the next story.

"Good ideas are those with which you most deeply connect. In deciding which story to write about, follow your intuitive feelings."

—Jewell Parker Rhodes, *Free Within Ourselves*

Questions:

- Are you brimming with story ideas already? Where do they come from? (If you aren't, don't worry!)

- How can you recognize your curiosity and lean into it?

- What could you do for an Artist's Date? Book one into your schedule soon.

- What fascinates you about people? How might those things turn into facets of character?

- What objects and artifacts interest you?

- What real events and places spark your curiosity?

- Consider the 'what if' questions behind the books you love, or other well-known books. How could you spin those in a new direction for your story?

- What quotes resonate with you?

- What themes and societal issues do you care about?
- What other books or myths or stories spark ideas for you?
- What aspects of your life could you mine for ideas?
- How will you capture your ideas?
- Are you worried about whether your ideas are unoriginal, or that someone will steal your ideas? If yes, how can you ease those fears?
- How will you choose which idea to work on?

Resources:

- *The Artist's Way: A Spiritual Path to Higher Creativity* — Julia Cameron
- *A Beautiful Anarchy: When the Life Creative Becomes the Life Created* — David duChemin
- *Big Magic: Creative Living Beyond Fear* — Elizabeth Gilbert
- *Free Within Ourselves: Fiction Lessons for Black Authors* — Jewell Parker Rhodes

"Do you have the courage to bring forth the treasures that are in you?"

—Elizabeth Gilbert, Big Magic

2.2 How to research your novel and when to stop

Don't write what you know. Write what you're interested in. That's always been my focus for fiction.

I love book research. It's one of the most fun parts of the creation process for me, but the danger is that you disappear down the research rabbit hole and forget to write the book, or you end up with so much research, you become overwhelmed and unable to make sense of it all.

Is research necessary?

Most fiction writers do some research, but the extent will differ depending on the book you're writing, and your personal preference. For example, a sprawling historical mystery set in 1800s London will require more research than a literary coming of age novel set in one house in the present day. A hard sci-fi epic series based on specific scientific discoveries will take more research than a stand-alone horror novel set in an underground bunker.

You can go into the research phase with no concrete agenda, as I often do, and find a story there somewhere. Or, if you have ideas already, research allows you to develop them further.

Most of my J.F. Penn thrillers are set in the present day, and I aim for accuracy in terms of settings and historical events that influence the plot. Then I push the edges of that reality into fiction and see what happens.

Readers of certain genres have expectations for research and accuracy. The reader wants to sink into your fictional world. If you introduce something that jolts them or rings untrue, you might get scathing reviews about errors in specific time periods, or the type of weapon or language a character uses. You can avoid these issues through research, but only you can decide how much you want to do.

How to research your novel

Research can take many forms. Here are three methods that yield good results for me.

(1) Read, watch, and listen

> "Books are made out of books."
> —Cormac McCarthy

When I get an inkling of an idea, my first step is usually to order and read a whole load of nonfiction books around the subject, or to visit a specialist library on the topic.

My crime thriller *Desecration* is set in modern-day London but the plot is based on the history of anatomy. I spent several months working in the Wellcome Collection library in Euston, London, which specializes in medical books.

While buying or borrowing books online is also a staple of my research process, I often find serendipity in the stacks of a physical library or bookshop. After all, we're book people. We love libraries!

You can also read magazines and journals, watch documentaries and films, or go down the rabbit hole on YouTube. You can fill the creative well in so many ways.

(2) Research through travel — real or virtual

Traveling is one of my favorite ways to research. Book-related travel might include going to another country, but it might also be another city, or visiting a museum or an art gallery. It usually involves physically going somewhere else, which helps me see things differently than if I am viewing them online. Of course, everyone has budget and time constraints, but I have never regretted a research trip and many of my novels are all the richer for my experiences in real life.

My thriller *Valley of Dry Bones* was several years in the making. I visited New Orleans in March 2017 and found a copy of the St Louis Bible at the back of the St Louis Cathedral in Jackson Square; on the same trip, I discovered the Spanish influence on the city.

Later that year, I visited Mission Dolores in San Francisco, where I found a statue of Junípero Serra, the eighteenth-century Spanish friar who founded the missions on the West Coast. I also went to Alcatraz, which appears in the climax of the book.

I followed the trail of history back to Spain, visiting Toledo for the original St Louis Bible, and Majorca, where Junípero Serra was born and raised. The final story combines voodoo and the Catholic church, and spans the history of the Spanish empire from West Africa to the USA.

On the cheaper end of the travel spectrum, exhibitions at the British Museum have inspired several of my stories. *Crypt of Bone* features an exhibition on religious relics. *Day of the Vikings* was — unsurprisingly — inspired by a Viking exhibition that included a sacred sword. My short story *The Dark Queen* was inspired by an exhibition called *Sunken Egypt*, and my character Blake Daniel from the Brooke and Daniel crime thrillers works at the museum as a researcher.

Of course, you can research many destinations online, so you can write about a place even if you haven't been there, or add layers to your story later. I use Google maps to ensure accuracy in locations, clips on YouTube to bring scenes to life, and travel blogs with photos to add a new angle to my writing. The pandemic encouraged even more museums, galleries, and collections to go online, so you can often find incredible resources to help with your story.

This type of research will become even easier once virtual reality (VR) headsets become more common, as they offer more immersive travel experiences without the crowds or the expense. While I hope this will never replace in-person travel completely, I certainly intend to use VR in my research process when it becomes more widely available.

(3) Research on Pinterest, Instagram, and other visual social media

Visual media can help you write about a place or find a setting that works well for your story, and you can also collect ideas for your books using Pinterest, Instagram, or other social media. Follow hashtags related to your story ideas and accounts that gather images on related topics.

I make Pinterest boards for my stories at:

www.pinterest.com/jfpenn

Worried about plagiarism?

Plagiarism is when you take someone else's work and pass it off as your own. Most authors would never consider doing this on purpose, but there is a possibility that it might happen accidentally. For example, you read and take notes on five books about the Tudors and then use that research directly within your novel without rephrasing. You could end up with lines from someone else's book in your own.

But don't worry. This is easy to avoid.

Make sure your note-taking process makes it clear when you copy someone else's words and when you paraphrase or write your own thoughts. Use quotation marks around quotes and never use those directly in your manuscript unless you attribute them.

Never copy and paste directly from your research notes into your manuscript. Always rewrite and rephrase.

When you're finished, you can also use a plagiarism checker like ProWritingAid to make sure you haven't unintentionally plagiarized. You'll find more on this topic in chapter 5.5 on useful tools.

When to stop researching

Research can be a lot of fun, but the more you research, the more information and ideas you will find. It can turn into a form of procrastination. At some point, you have to start writing the book.

You don't have to do all the research before you write. You can research enough to get started and then do mini-research dives when you need to fill in the blanks. This is my process as part of discovery. I often don't know what I need to research until I get to that point in the story.

Balance consumption and creation, input and output.

If you're struggling with knowing when to stop, consider a time limit. Set a date to start the actual writing, then work backward to allow yourself an initial research period. You can always do additional research as you write.

Should you use an Author's Note about your research?

As a reader, I love an Author's Note, so naturally, I include them at the end of my novels along with a bibliography.

I include notes on research and historical accuracy, as well as links to a Pinterest board for each book with images that inspired the setting. It's certainly not required, but my readers often comment that they enjoy seeing where my ideas came from and even researching areas further.

Research and synchronicity in action

One of my favorite parts of the research process is synchronicity — things that are coincidental in a meaningful way, that emerge unexpectedly, and underscore why this story is right. An encouragement from the Muse, perhaps.

When I started my ARKANE thriller *End of Days*,

I only had the title in mind. I knew it would feature some kind of apocalyptic event, but I also wanted to have an original angle on what is a common theme.

I read some books on biblical prophecy and how different religions see the end of the world, and gathered a wealth of ideas. One particular Bible verse from Revelation 20 intrigued me:

"Then I saw an angel coming down from heaven holding in his hand the key to the bottomless pit and a great chain. And he sees the dragon, that ancient serpent who is the devil and Satan and bound him for a thousand years and threw him into the pit, and shut it and sealed it over him until the thousand years were ended."

That sparked a story question. What if the thousand years were ended? What would happen to that serpent in the pit?

I love including art and architecture in my novels, so I googled art associated with serpents. I discovered Lilith, the first wife of Adam, also considered a demon associated with serpents.

The Jewish Talmud says of Lilith, "The female of Samael is called 'serpent, woman of harlotry, end of all flesh, end of days.'"

Yes, the Talmud actually calls her the End of Days.

When this kind of synchronicity happens, I know I'm on the right track with a story. It happens with every novel I write at some point, and it's part of why I love the research discovery process. Lilith and Samael became the antagonists in *End of Days*.

I found an amazing documentary on YouTube about Appalachian snake-handling churches, which I wove into Lilith's back story. I discovered the 'bottomless pit' in the Marianas Trench in the Pacific Ocean, and from there, the plot of the novel developed, along with the characters and the inevitable climax in Jerusalem. No spoilers!

* * *

Some kind of research will be necessary for your novel. You get to decide how to approach it in the way that suits you and your story.

Whether it sparks initial ideas or is wound into every chapter, the time invested in research will ultimately deliver rewards in terms of the quality of your finished book and reader satisfaction. But remember, stop researching and start writing at some point!

Questions:

- Do you enjoy research? How could you make research part of your writing process?
- What kinds of research will you do for your book?
- How can you avoid plagiarism?
- How will you know when to stop researching?

Resources:

- *Books Are Made Out of Books: A Guide to Cormac McCarthy's Literary Influences* — Michael Lynn Crews
- *Research Like A Librarian: Research Help and Tips for Writers for Researching in the Digital Age* — Vikki J. Carter, The Author's Librarian
- *Steal Like An Artist: 10 Things Nobody Told You About Being Creative* — Austin Kleon
- Interview on research with Vikki J. Carter, The Author's Librarian — www.thecreativepenn.com/2021/10/18/how-to-research-your-book-authors-librarian/
- ProWritingAid Plagiarism Checker — www.TheCreativePenn.com/prowritingaid

2.3 Outlining (or plotting)

> "Outlining is the most efficient way to structure a novel to achieve the greatest emotional impact… Outlining lets you create a framework that compels your audience to keep reading from the first page to the last."
>
> —*Jeffery Deaver*

Writers who outline or plot spend more time up front considering aspects of the novel and know how the story will progress before they start writing the manuscript. It's a spectrum, with some outlines consisting of a page or so and others stretching to thousands of words of preparation.

The benefits of outlining

While discovery writers jump into writing and spend more time later cleaning up their drafts, outliners or plotters spend time beforehand so they can write faster in the first draft.

When it's time to write, outliners focus on writing words on the page to fulfil their vision rather than figuring out what's going on. Outlining can result in more intricate plots and twists, deeper characters, less time rewriting, and faster production time.

If you co-write, outlining is the only way to ensure your process works smoothly. As a discovery writer, I have found it particularly challenging to co-write fiction, which is why I rarely do it!

If you have an agent or a publisher, or you *want* an agent or a publisher, you might have to write an outline anyway, so learning how to do it well can help. If you're a discovery writer, you can always outline after the book is finished, if you need to.

> "When you plan a story the right way, you guarantee a tight, compelling structure that keeps readers turning pages and delivers a satisfying reading experience from start to finish. And really, a satisfied reader is all you need for a 'good' book."
>
> —Libbie Hawker, *Take Off Your Pants! Outline Your Books for Faster, Better Writing*

The difficulties of outlining

Outlining and plotting suit some writers very well.

But not all.

Some authors get lost in outlining and plotting and world-building and character bios and theme explorations and symbolism… and never actually write full sentences and may never finish a book.

Such writers may go astray through a combination of procrastination through preparation, a delight in the learning process without a desire to do the work to turn it into a story, or perhaps fear of what might happen if they do write.

Some authors outline a book and then decide it's too boring to write it and never finish.

Some authors become so obsessed with the technicalities of outlining that they decide writing is too hard, so they give up.

Other writers try outlining only to find it is no fun at all.

If you can do it, brilliant!

If you can't, don't worry. See the next chapter on discovery writing.

How to outline

> "Every hour spent outlining prior to starting a novel saves you many hours in the actual writing process. It also helps you to write a better novel, as you will 'tighten' down the story in your outline before you write, rather than having to do it in rewrite."
>
> —Bob Mayer, *The Novel Writer's Toolkit*

There is no single way to outline, but options include a text document, a spreadsheet, mind maps, and/or Scrivener or other software. Outlines can also vary in length and complexity.

Shawn Coyne describes the Foolscap Method in *The Story Grid*, where an entire book can be outlined on one A4 page with just a few lines describing the beginning, middle, and end of the story.

You could expand this brief outline into a document of a few pages by describing the main action points and characters of each scene in a couple of lines or a paragraph. This is often what agents and publishers mean by an outline.

At the more extreme end of the plotting spectrum, thriller author Jeffery Deaver creates a lengthy outline for his thrillers. As he said in a *Wall Street Journal* interview in 2012, "The finished outline runs about 150 pages, single spaced, though with very wide right margins, so I can jot references to the research material relevant to the plot."

James Patterson outlines his books and uses the process to complicate his plots and come up with twists that surprise readers. Patterson is a prolific story machine and works with co-writers to expand his story worlds. Whatever you think of his books, he is the highest-earning and bestselling author in the world. I highly recommend his MasterClass online course, in which he goes into detail about his process.

In the MasterClass, Patterson says, "I'm a fanatic about outlining. It's going to make whatever you're writing better. You'll have fewer false starts and you'll take a shorter amount of time. I write them over and over again. You read my outline and it's like reading a book. You really get the story even though it's condensed. Each chapter will have about a paragraph devoted to it, but you're going to get the scene and you're going to get the sense of what makes the scene work… The ending almost always changes in the writing, though, it's because I learned to listen to the characters."

Some writers use paper index cards for plotting scenes and characters. Lauren Beukes used a wall of index cards to physically plot the details for her award-winning thriller *The Shining Girls*, later adapted for TV. It is a time travel thriller, so the plot lines and characters needed to be interwoven in multiple ways.

If you don't want to use paper, you can use plotting software like Scrivener, Plottr, Granthika, or other tools to create electronic versions of index cards that you can drag and drop into a different order as you need to.

J.K. Rowling outlined the *Harry Potter* series with hand-drawn matrices tracking the characters against the plot and timeline.

Prolific thriller author Russell Blake uses a spreadsheet with chapter numbers down the left, character names across the top, and a few sentences in each cell. "I will typically capture the whys of the chapter, meaning the motivation for writing it. To make it into my final outline, it will need to either reveal something about the characters or the plot, or move the story forward. If I can't articulate to myself the purpose of the chapter in that manner, I cut it."

You can include whatever you like in your outline and it can be as long as you want it to be.

Outliners often change things as they write, so don't feel that the outline is a constraint on your creativity. It's just a tool to help you write your book in whatever way works for you.

> "A good outline should be a spur for creativity, not a stumbling block. The author is the master of the outline, not its slave."
>
> —K.M. Weiland, *Outlining Your Novel*

Outlining a series

If you have a series in mind, particularly if there is a clear character arc and a final ending, then it can be a good idea to outline more than one book at the same time so you know where the series is going, even if it's just a few lines.

However, remember to write the book at some point. Don't spend forever outlining!

Questions:

- What are the benefits of outlining?
- What are the potential difficulties?
- Are you excited about the prospect of outlining? Or is it something you feel like you 'should' do?
- Which methods of outlining might work best for you?
- How much time do you want to spend outlining before you move on to writing?

Resources:

- "How J.K. Rowling Plotted *Harry Potter* with a Hand-Drawn Spreadsheet," Open Culture — www.openculture.com/2014/07/j-k-rowling-plotted-harry-potter-with-a-hand-drawn-spreadsheet.html
- "Outlining made simple," Russell Blake's blog — www.russellblake.com/outlining-made-simple
- "String Theory and Murder Walls," Lauren Beukes's blog — www.laurenbeukes.com/string-theory-and-murder-walls

- "The Architecture of a Thriller" by Jeffery Deaver, *Wall Street Journal*, 15 June 2012 — www.wsj.com/articles/SB10001424052702303734204577464681207430076

- *Outlining Your Novel: Map Your Way to Success* — K.M. Weiland

- *Take Off Your Pants! Outline Your Books for Faster, Better Writing* — Libbie Hawker

- *The Novel Writer's Toolkit: From Idea to Best-Seller* — Bob Mayer

2.4 Discovery writing (or pantsing)

> "If you surrender to the wind, you can ride it."
>
> —Toni Morrison, *Song of Solomon*

The term 'pantsing' comes from the term 'fly by the seat of your pants,' and essentially means that you write what comes into your head and work out the story along the way.

For some people, this means literally starting from the first sentence of the first page and writing until the story is done. For others, it involves writing out of order and stitching the story together later, which is my approach.

Let's first address the term 'pantsing,' which is frankly terrible! It's based on the American word 'pants,' meaning trousers, but I'm British, and pants are underwear. I much prefer the term 'discovery writing,' so that's what I'll use and perhaps together we can get rid of the term 'pantsing' altogether.

The benefits of discovery writing

It's so much fun!

Many discovery writers feel as if knowing what happens or planning it all in advance makes the writing process boring, but if you don't know what will happen next in your story, the writing process has the intensity and excitement of discovery. This can make the finished product just as interesting for the reader as it was for you in the writing process.

I also find these extraordinary moments of synchronicity happen when I discovery write and research as I go. They happen during the writing of every book, although I can't force them to happen. There's a moment where the story clicks, it all suddenly makes sense, and things that I invented cross over into the real world in unexpected ways. That feeling makes the creative potential of the discovery process almost addictive.

You need to have a certain amount of trust in your innate story sense, but that is also part of the enjoyment. We have all read so many books and watched so many movies and TV shows that we have a deep understanding of story as human beings. There's a sense of 'knowing' how a story works, and in discovery writing, it's about leaning into this feeling.

Trust that your subconscious story brain will give you what you need along the way.

> "Writing with intentional plot structure is not necessary for the story to be compelling."
>
> —Becca Syme & Susan Bischoff,
> *Dear Writer, Are You Intuitive?*

The difficulties of discovery writing

If you don't know how the story will work, you can end up writing yourself into a corner. Many discovery writers discard words, scenes, characters, and plot points later. Some may have to redraft altogether to make a story work. Some consider that a 'waste,' but it's just part of the discovery process.

You will also face the blank page regularly in your writing sessions, as you might not always know what to write next.

Dean Wesley Smith addresses this in *Writing into The Dark*: "Getting stuck is part of writing into the dark. It is… a natural part of the process of a creative voice building a story. Embrace the uncertainty of being stuck, trust your creative voice, give it a few moments' rest, and then come back and write the next sentence."

Reframe the blank page as the promise of unlimited possibility, rather than the fear of the unknown.

How to discovery write

> "Story emerges from human minds as naturally as breath emerges from between human lips. You don't have to be a genius to master it. You're already doing it."
>
> —Will Storr, *The Science of Storytelling*

Write a sentence.

Then another one.

Then another one.

Repeat until done for the writing session.

You don't have to tell the story in a linear fashion. You can jump around and write what the Muse wants to write and piece it all together later. That's how it works for me. I never write in order.

When you sit down to discovery write, you need to trust that something will emerge from you somehow, even if it feels like you have nothing when you face the blank page.

Of course, you must learn the craft. There must be an element of understanding the principles of story.

But there is also something ineffable, something unexplainable, something magic that happens when you trust the discovery process.

You may not even realize what is in your consciousness until it spills onto the page. As poet Ben Okri said, we are "magnificent and mysterious beings capable of creating civilisations out of the wild lands of the earth and the dark places in our consciousness."

As Walt Whitman said, "I am large, I contain multitudes."

You can do this. Trust emergence.

Authors who are discovery writers

Lee Child used to start writing his next Jack Reacher thriller on 1 September each year and continue writing until the book was done (before he handed the franchise over to his brother in 2020). In an interview with *Marie Claire* magazine, he said, "I just start somewhere, somewhere that feels good, and then literally think 'Alright now what happens?' So a million times in the process it's a question of

'Alright now what happens?' and so the story tells itself."

I'm a Jack Reacher fan and the storylines are linear and work well for this kind of writing style. Reacher arrives in a town, something bad happens, he must find and punish the bad guys, and there's some fighting and (occasionally) some loving along the way. There is a clear protagonist, and the story unfolds in real time as Reacher experiences it.

But not everyone writes such a linear story and you certainly don't have to.

Stephen King is a discovery writer and his books are usually sprawling stories with many characters, multiple points of view, and often a complicated plot. In *On Writing*, he talks about starting with a character in a situation and writing from there. "Stories are found things, like fossils in the ground," which must be uncovered through the writing process. King does multiple drafts and revisions to deepen the story, but his first draft is all discovery. He says, "I believe plotting and the spontaneity of real creation aren't compatible."

Tess Gerritsen talks about her discovery process in an article on her blog: "Since I don't outline ahead of time, I don't always know the solution to the mystery. So I'll wander in the wilderness along with my characters until I get about two-thirds of the way through and I'll be forced to find answers. And then I can finally write to the end... I don't stop to revise during the first draft. Because it's all going to be changed anyway, when I finally figure out what the book is about."

Nora Roberts says in a blog post about her method: "The first draft, the discovery draft, the POS (guess what that stands for) draft is the hardest for me. Figuring it all out, creating people I'm going to care about enough to sit here with hours every day in order to tell their story. Finding out information about the setting, the careers involved, and so much more. I don't outline. I have a kind of loose mental outline, then I sit down, get started and hope it all works one more time."

Dean Wesley Smith has written several hundred novels and shares his process in *Writing into the Dark: How to Write a Novel Without an Outline*. He talks about 'cycling,' where he writes a scene and then cycles back to read through it and make changes as necessary every time he sits down to write. He might deepen the character or add to the plot, or make other changes. Sometimes he might find a plot issue and have to cycle back further, but when he finishes the first full draft, the book is done. He has a proofreader check it and then publishes.

My process: Discovery writing with a touch of plotting

I have tried so many times to become an outliner. I've read all the books on structure and plotting and done lots of courses, but my Muse just won't comply. It frankly makes me miserable to try and outline in any detail. My creative brain just doesn't work that way. It sucks the joy out of the writing process — and what's the point in that?!

I have written and published many novels at this point, so clearly my process works, even if it doesn't fit neatly into the way many others say we 'should' write. This is how I discovery write.

I have various ideas mulling around in my head for a long time before I start a book. They might be ideas about a character, a setting, a story question, a theme I want to explore, or a MacGuffin — an object of a quest (all of which I'll cover later, in Part 3).

I have a folder on my computer in my J.F. Penn drive with sub-folders labelled with broad-brush working titles. Most of the folders are empty, but they are placeholders for the Muse. As I write this, I have sixteen folders in my To Write list, but they are pretty nebulous. For example, Volcano Botanist Adventure, and French Gothic Stonemason. I have vague ideas about what these stories might be some day, but they take years to emerge. I move the folders up and down depending on how I'm feeling about what I might write next.

At some point, I settle on the story I need to write. That decision is driven by an urging from the Muse, or something external that triggers the choice, like a research trip where a story piece clicks into place.

I don't write to a production schedule for my fiction and I have spectacularly failed to plan when my books might come out. I am incredibly organized in my nonfiction side as Joanna Penn and in my business, but my fiction self — my J.F. Penn side — cannot be constrained. This is why I don't do long pre-orders on my fiction. I only ever put a pre-order up when the book is with my editor, as then I know the timeline for publication.

I'll spend some time researching and, at the point of committing to a book, I usually have at least a character idea and sometimes a name, a setting for the opening scene, and ideas for what the plot might be about. But most of the time, I haven't written any of it down. Sometimes, I draw a mind map in my journal. Sometimes I have the equivalent of an A4 piece of paper with thoughts, but it's all pretty free-flowing.

I open a new Scrivener project and add some placeholders for scenes. These are just one liners. For example, in *Destroyer of Worlds*, my first placeholder line was: 'Trafalgar Square bomb, something stolen from the ARKANE vault.' I didn't know what was stolen, but that emerged once I sat down to write.

I schedule first-draft blocks of time in my calendar. I turn up at my desk or the writing café or wherever I'm working and I write.

I don't write in order. I write whatever scene comes to mind that day, or whatever is suggested as the next scene based on what I have already written. I might follow one character for a few scenes and then go back and write another timeline later. I add more placeholder one-liners as the plot emerges.

I research before I begin, but I also research as I write. For example, when writing a scene set in Cologne Cathedral for *Tomb of Relics*, I had the cathedral interactive site open so I could write as if

I was actually there. I also check aspects of plot as I type. Yes, sometimes I end up down a rabbit hole during the draft, but that's okay too, because there's gold in the research process for a discovery writer!

I don't do character profiles. My characters emerge from the discovery writing process. I'll often write a scene to expand on character motivations and back story later in the process, but then insert it earlier in the story. This is why I love writing in Scrivener. I can drag and drop and reorder my scenes as I go.

When I get to around 20,000 words of a full-length novel, I often lose track of what's going on with the different threads of the story. I usually stop and reread what I have so far, noting down open questions, character issues, plot holes, and anything else. This process helps me figure out what else needs to happen, and I can usually write to the end after this reread. I can also use dictation at this point in the process as I know more about what's going on, but it doesn't usually work for me earlier in the discovery process, as I only know what I will write as I type.

My first self-edit is when I structure scenes into chapters and find what I need to cut and add — often that leads to a major reorganization of the material. It's all part of the discovery process.

* * *

There are as many different ways of writing as there are writers, but we all end up with a finished book regardless of how we get there. You have to find the process that works for you.

Questions:

- What are the benefits of discovery writing?
- What are the potential difficulties?
- Are you excited about the prospect of discovery writing? Does the empty page scare you or represent unlimited possibility?
- How do you think discovery writing might fit into your process?

Resources:

- *Dear Writer, Are You Intuitive?*
  — Becca Syme and Susan Bischoff

- *On Writing: A Memoir of the Craft*
  — Stephen King

- *The Science of Storytelling: Why Stories Make Us Human, and How To Tell Them Better*
  — Will Storr

- *Writing into the Dark: How to Write a Novel Without an Outline* — Dean Wesley Smith

- *Mental Fight* — Ben Okri

- *Song of Myself* — Walt Whitman

- *Song of Solomon* — Toni Morrison

- "Jack Reacher author Lee Child on why he never plots his novels," *Marie Claire*, November 2018 — www.marieclaire.co.uk/entertainment/books/jack-reacher-author-lee-child-never-plots-novel-628396

- "Doing it," Tess Gerritsen's blog — web.archive.org/web/20150912064617/https://www.tessgerritsen.com/doing-it/

- "Here's how I work," Nora Roberts's blog — fallintothestory.com/heres-how-i-work/

"If you surrender to the wind, you can ride it."

—Toni Morrison,
Song of Solomon

2.5 What are you writing? Genre

Genre is about understanding where your story fits. It's also about reader expectation.

Many first-time writers think their book is for 'everybody.'

But it's not.

Readers like different kinds of books, and that's a good thing. It means that it's likely you will find a market for whatever you write, however distinctive.

Some authors declare they do not want to be constrained by genre and refuse to be boxed in by story convention or reader expectation.

That's fine. Write whatever you want to.

But if you intend to publish your book, either through the traditional or the independent author route, you're going to have to get to grips with categorizing it at some point.

Genre is just another word for category

Think about a bookstore — your favorite physical store or wherever you shop online.

Every book fits into that ecosystem somehow. Every book has to be shelved somewhere, and with online stores, each book can be virtually shelved in multiple places.

Replace the word 'genre' with 'category' and it's clear that every book has one, or more than one.

There are also sub-categories. Fantasy is a genre or a category, but my husband only reads epic fantasy. He loves really long series in the classic style of Tolkien, whereas I prefer dark fantasy, which blends fantasy with supernatural horror, and urban fantasy, which often features fantastical elements in a contemporary setting.

Literary fiction is a genre or category, too, and also has its own sub-categories. For example, historical literary fiction like *Wolf Hall* by Hilary Mantel, or speculative fiction like *Frankenstein* by Mary Shelley, or literary fantasy like *Black Leopard, Red Wolf* by Marlon James.

Some authors know what genre they want to write

before they begin. For my first novel, I knew I wanted to create a fast-paced thriller with religious elements in the style of Dan Brown's *The Da Vinci Code*. That's the kind of book I read on the commuter train to the day job I hated. I loved escaping into an adventure that spanned cultural and religious locations and themes, and that's the experience I wanted to provide for my readers.

For some of my other books, I only figured out the genre later, so don't worry if you're not sure what you want to write, or what genre your book might be. Many authors don't understand their genre until much later in the process.

How can understanding genre help you as an author?

Knowing your genre can help you with the writing process. If you write in a genre you love and have been reading for years, you already understand the reader expectations. You know what a satisfying read feels like, and you want to elicit that feeling in your readers.

What makes a story satisfying for you? Think of your favorite books, movies, and TV shows. Why are they so satisfying? What do you love about them?

If you understand the conventions of the genre, you can include aspects that readers expect and love in your story.

In a traditional romance, there is a 'meet-cute' scene where the two characters encounter each other for the first time. They are often thrown together under difficult circumstances and there is conflict to overcome from the start. If you love romance, you know how this story should progress.

The characters face difficulties and must figure out their conflict; eventually, there will be a happy ending.

In the thrillers I love, there will always be a scene where the hero is at the mercy of the villain. Consider the classic James Bond movie, *Goldfinger*.

Bond is strapped to a table, and a laser is about to cut him in half.

"Do you expect me to talk?"

"No, Mr Bond, I expect you to die."

How will Bond get out of this situation?

It looks like all is lost, but fans of the genre know this scene is necessary. After the character hits rock bottom, they will figure their way out of danger and eventually triumph.

Understanding genre and reader expectations can also help you market your book. If you can write a story that pleases readers, your book will sell, however you choose to publish. It will be easier to pitch to agents, it will be easier to self-publish, it will be easier to create the right book cover, and it will be easier to market. So if you do know in advance, it can certainly help.

How do you figure out what genre you're writing?

It might be simple to figure out the broad category.

If your story has a spaceship or an alien, it's probably science-fiction. But of course, there are so many variations within science-fiction, you will need to delve a little deeper.

Is it a romance with a love story that unfolds across a journey into the stars?

Is it a dystopian, post-apocalyptic adventure where the characters escape a dying Earth?

Is it a horror story where an ancient alien species intends to destroy the human race?

If you're still struggling, find at least five books that are like the one you're writing. None of them will match exactly, but you should be able to find a few that you can use as comparison titles.

If you can't find any immediately, then try reading more widely. Search for lists of books on Google and I guarantee you will find more options.

I searched for 'mermaid horror' and found a list of 'evil mermaid' books on Goodreads with more suggestions. Yes, this is a thing! (If this sub-genre intrigues you, try *Into the Drowning Deep* by Mira Grant and *All the Murmuring Bones* by Angela Slatter, both excellent!)

Once you have your list, search for each book on Amazon. Scroll down to the Product Details and look at the categories it is shelved in.

For example, *The Source* by James Michener is listed under:

- Genre Fiction — Historical — Jewish
- Genre Fiction — Family Saga

It's pretty clear what you can expect from reading the book and, indeed, it is an epic historical saga stretching across generations of a Jewish family in Israel.

If you follow this process for books that are similar

to what you're writing, you'll get a clearer idea of your possible genre/s.

You can do this by manual searching, but you can also use the program Publisher Rocket to research genre categories in more depth.

Won't genre conventions make my story generic?

Short answer. No.

How many times have you read about two people who fall in love?

How many times have you read about mothers and sons, or fathers and daughters?

How many times have you read about characters who overcome evil and save the world?

Your story will be original because of the characters you create and the detail you bring to every element within whatever genre you write in.

What if I write cross-genre?

Great! If you read cross-genre, you're likely to write cross-genre, and readers love these books, too.

My Brooke and Daniel thrillers span crime, psychological thriller, and supernatural thriller categories. They don't appeal to fans of straight police procedurals, which rarely have supernatural elements, but those who enjoy cross-genre novels in this vein rate them highly.

If you self-publish, you can categorize your book into ten different sub-categories, so you can virtually shelve your book in multiple ways.

What is writing to market?

> "Writing to market is picking an underserved genre that you know has a voracious appetite and then giving that market exactly what it wants."
>
> —Chris Fox, Write to Market

Some authors set out to write a novel aimed at a particular target market. They construct the story around reader expectations and genre conventions, while adding their creative spin to set it apart.

This approach suits the outliner far more than the discovery writer as you need to know what you're aiming for from the beginning.

Writing to market doesn't guarantee commercial

success or critical acclaim, but some writers swear by this method and many of them are incredibly successful. You have to decide for yourself what kind of process suits you.

I spent thirteen years doing a job I hated and when I left it to become a full-time author entrepreneur in 2011, I wanted freedom of time and freedom of creative choice. As a discovery writer, I follow my Muse into my story and write fiction that engages me first; I only figure out where the books fit once they are finished. I certainly make less money with my fiction than some authors who write to market, but I love my creative process. It suits me and my lifestyle.

There is no right way. You will make your choice per project and per book.

What if I'm writing in a 'dead' genre?

After the success of *The Hunger Games*, everyone seemed to be writing YA (young adult) dystopian fiction. After the success of *Gone Girl*, psychological thrillers with unreliable female narrators became the next big thing. And of course, *Fifty Shades of Grey* was responsible for a resurgence in erotica.

The 'hot' genres will always have their day and then

the media declares them dead. Agents might not want to acquire books in that genre anymore, preferring whatever the new emerging genre might be.

But readers love what they love. They will continue to seek books that satisfy them, regardless of traditional media's opinion that the genre is hot or not. Independent authors often make a living in genres rejected by the traditional industry because no genre is ever dead while readers keep demanding more stories.

Vampires are a classic example of a supposedly dead genre that keeps coming back again and again. *Interview with a Vampire* by Anne Rice was published in 1976 and made into a film with Tom Cruise and Brad Pitt in 1994. With *Twilight* in 2005, vampire mania circled around again, and if you love a good vampire novel, there are many more variations on the classic trope than ever before. Vampire fans have more than enough to read, and if you love the genre, you will never want for readers.

Questions:

- How can understanding genre help you as an author?

- Do you know what genre you're writing in? Don't worry if you don't, but perhaps you already have some idea.

- What makes a satisfying story for you? Think of your top five books, as well as your favorite movies and/or TV shows. Why are they so satisfying? What do you love about them?

- Choose five to ten books that are like what you're writing, which may be different from the books chosen above. Research their categories on Amazon. Are there commonalities? Might you be writing cross-genre?

- What genre conventions might your novel include?

- Is writing to market something you're interested in? Why?

- If your favorite genre has been declared 'dead', what elements could you add, tweak, or subvert to make it feel fresh?

Resources:

- *The Story Grid: What Good Editors Know*
  — Shawn Coyne

- *Write to Market: Deliver a Book That Sells*
  — Chris Fox

- Publisher Rocket software for analyzing books, categories, and keywords
  — www.TheCreativePenn.com/rocket

- Publisher Rocket tutorial
  — www.TheCreativePenn.com/rocket-tutorial

- K-lytics genre reports and analysis for top selling genres and sub-categories
  — www.TheCreativePenn.com/genre

2.6 What are you writing? Short story, novella, or novel

Many new writers ask how long their story should be. There are two approaches to figuring out the best answer:

(A) Start with your target word count and construct the story within those constraints.

For example, you want to write a 90,000-word thriller to submit to agents, or a 3,000-word short story for a competition with specific word count guidelines.

(B) Start writing and see what it turns into.

There might only be enough in your idea for a short story, or it might expand into a wide-ranging novel of over 120,000 words. You might not know which it is until you get started, especially if you are a discovery writer.

Both methods are valid, and you will probably use both along your author journey.

There are, however, some rough guidelines for word count, although each category can vary depending on the situation.

Flash fiction is under 1,000 words.

Short stories range from 2,000 to 5,000 words. If you're submitting to an anthology, a specific publication, or a competition, they will specify word count.

Novellas range from 20,000 to 40,000 words.

Novels are anything over 50,000 words, and length will vary by genre and reader expectations. Romance is often closer to 50,000 words with thrillers, crime, and mystery usually around 70,000 to 90,000 words. Beware of writing an epic fantasy under 120,000 words!

Go back to your list of books like the one you aim to write. Check the page count and assume around 300 words per page. Multiply together to get a rough estimate of the number of words in the book.

IT by Stephen King is a doorstopper of a book with 1,088 pages in the paperback version — over 300,000 words for what is a sprawling, coming-of-age, epic horror novel.

Mrs Dalloway by Virginia Woolf is a slim 108 pages,

around 32,000 words, making it a literary women's fiction novella.

Questions:

- Do you know the length of the story you want to write?
- Go back to your list of comparison books. How long are they? What is the reader expectation in the genre?

2.7 What are you writing? Stand-alone, series, or serial

Another consideration for your story is whether it exists as a stand-alone, or if it stretches across multiple books in a series, or if it's an ongoing story delivered as a serial.

Again, you might not know this up front, and for discovery writers, stories can have a will of their own!

When I wrote *Map of Shadows*, I thought it was a stand-alone story, but after I finished the book, there was more to tell. While I had resolved the initial story arc, I couldn't leave my characters where they were.

Then I thought it was an episodic series, with the main characters having fresh adventures through different maps in each book, so I wrote book two, *Map of Plagues*, with that in mind.

But once I was midway through book three, *Map of the Impossible*, a bittersweet ending emerged and it became a trilogy. I can write more in that world, but there was a clear end to the main story arc.

Yes, it would have been much more organized and simpler to have designed it as a trilogy in the first place, but that's the joy of discovery writing!

Stand-alone

A stand-alone novel is a satisfying story with a clear ending for the characters that ties up any loose endings in the plot. There is no need for another book. The story is complete.

Stand-alones are more common in some genres than others. For example, horror and speculative fiction are often stand-alone novels. *The Deep* by Michaelbrent Collings is an underwater supernatural horror novel, and a perfect example of a stand-alone in my opinion.

My dark fantasy, coming-of-age, supernatural thriller *Risen Gods*, co-written with J. Thorn, is also a stand-alone.

With a stand-alone, you can reinvent your world and characters every time and explore different sub-genres over time — giving you a better chance of writing something that readers love. But this ability to experiment is also the major drawback because stand-alones can take longer to write as you start afresh every time. There is also no sell-through to the next book in the series, so stand-alones might make you less income overall.

Series

If your characters return in more than one book within the same genre and in the same world, then the books are a series. Readers love series because they can sink into a world and spend time with characters they love again and again.

There are different types of series. There are episodic, progressive series; for example, detective mysteries and police procedurals have key characters who work together to solve different crimes in each book.

My ARKANE thrillers are episodic adventures. Morgan and Jake and the ARKANE team solve a different supernatural mystery — and stop the baddies destroying the world! — in every book.

You can also have linked characters in a series where the stories are not episodic; for example, the Bridgerton historical romance series by Julia Quinn follows each sibling in the Bridgerton family. My mum writes sweet romance under the pen name Penny Appleton, and each character has a link to the English village of Summerfield.

There are also series with a long arc but a clear ending, common in epic fantasies like George R.R. Martin's *A Song of Ice and Fire*, of which *A Game of Thrones* is book one. (Although, as I write this, the TV adaptation is complete but the novel series is still ongoing.)

In terms of benefits, you don't have to invent a new world and new characters every time, so subsequent books in a series can be faster to write. Series books are easier to market as you can use promotions on the first one, and authors who write in a series often make more money over time because readers buy all the subsequent books if they're engaged with the story.

However, one drawback is that you might spend many books developing a series only to find it doesn't resonate with the market. Or, if the series is successful, you may feel trapped by the reader expectation to write more in that world.

Serial

Serial fiction is nothing new. Charles Dickens published most of his novels as serials, selling individual parts or including them in the magazines he edited, which accounts for the length of his books and also the memorable characters that kept readers coming back for more each time.

Serial reading has become much more popular in the digital age, offered through apps like Wattpad, Radish, Kindle Vella, and other services. These micro-reading experiences keep a reader hooked and ready for the next installment — one major benefit of this form. Some of the best serial writers, particularly in Asia, write long-running serials that continue far beyond the word count of most book series.

However, serial writing is a particular skill with a focus on cliff-hangers and open loops. Read a lot of it if you want to write it.

Which is the best option?

Only you can decide for your story, but consider what you like to read as a good starting point.

I don't read serial fiction, so I don't write it, regardless of its popularity. I love reading long-running episodic thriller series, so most of my writing takes that form. I also read a lot of stand-alone horror and speculative fiction books, as well as short stories, so those formats shape other aspects of what I write.

If you're thinking ahead to publication, and you want to consider the more commercial aspects of writing, it is definitely easier to market a series, and if you get a traditional publishing deal, they may want more than one book. So even if you write a stand-alone, consider how some characters might continue beyond this story.

Questions:

- What kind of stories do you read? Revisit your favorite books and also those that are like what you're writing. Are they stand-alone, series, or serial?

- What kind of story are you writing? How would it be different as a stand-alone, a series, or a serial. Why are you choosing one format over another? (And if you don't know yet, don't worry, you can figure it out along the way).

Resources:

- *How to Write a Series: A Guide to Series Types and Structure plus Troubleshooting Tips and Marketing Tactics* — Sara Rosett

- *Romance Your Brand: Building a Marketable Genre Fiction Series* — Zoe York

- Interview on how to write a series, with seven-figure fantasy author Lindsay Buroker — www.TheCreativePenn.com/writeseries

Part 3: Aspects of a Novel

3.1 Story structure

> "I do not over-intellectualize the production process. I try to keep it simple: Tell the damned story."
>
> —*Tom Clancy*

On one level, we know instinctively what makes a good story. We read and watch favorite books and movies again and again because they leave us satisfied. We also know when a story doesn't work. Either the ending strikes the wrong note, or we leave it partway through because we are just not hooked in.

We understand story at this instinctive level because we've been mainlining it our entire lives—from picture books in childhood, to the Netflix series we binge-watched last weekend, to the novel we had to read in one sitting because it wouldn't let us go.

Despite all this story instinct, it's still difficult to put thoughts into words, to turn your ideas into a finished novel that someone else will enjoy.

Pages of writing are not a story, and it takes more than a lot of words to satisfy a reader.

You need to understand basic story structure — but don't drown in it

When I started to work on this project, I revisited some of the (many) books I've read on story structure. I also have journals full of notes from workshops and online courses.

I found myself quickly drowning in way too much material.

You can get so lost in these books that you forget why you wanted to write in the first place. Perhaps you even lose the excitement for your story through over-analysis.

Of course, your reaction will depend on your creative preference and personality. Analytical writers, plotters, and outliners, might resonate with detailed structure, while discovery writers might prefer to write more organically and restructure later as necessary.

Once again, it doesn't matter. We all end up with a finished manuscript at some point. Story structure is essential, even if you figure it out later in the process.

My goal with this book is to simplify concepts as much as possible and help you finish your novel, so I've focused on basic story structure here. If you want to explore further, I've listed many additional books in the Resources.

But remember the iceberg.

You need to know enough to finish this novel, but you don't need to know everything before you write it.

Simplified story structure 1: Five elements

Let's start with something super simple. In her book on outlining, *Take Off Your Pants*, Libbie Hawker says, "Every compelling story has the following five elements:

1) A character

2) The character wants something

3) But something prevents him from getting what
he wants easily

4) So he struggles against that force

5) And either succeeds or fails.

Fill in the details and you will have a story.

Simplified story structure 2: Three-act structure

At a high level, the typical three-act structure is simply a beginning, a middle, and an end.

This structure is nothing new. It goes all the way back to Aristotle's *Poetics* and the Greek tragedies of over two thousand years ago, and is still used as the basis for many of the best-selling story structure books today.

Three-act structure resonates so deeply because it is similar to the way the stories of our lives progress.

In life, you have a beginning, you have a long middle full of challenges, and then you have an end.

On a smaller scale, each day begins with morning routines, then you get on with whatever you do for the day, then you return home and have evening rituals before bed. If you think about it that way, the three-act structure is not so complicated. Once you know it and understand it, then you can play with the rules.

> **Act 1:** The story starts in the ordinary world of the character, then the inciting incident happens to kick-start the story.

Act 2: This is the bulk of the novel.

There is rising action and conflict, complication, and progressively more difficulty. The stakes rise. The character tries to get what they want, fails, and keeps trying and failing. They may enlist help from other characters, but things get really bad at some point.

Act 3: In the climax, the story reaches its peak, and the character achieves their goal or fails, depending on the genre. The story questions and subplots are resolved. There is a satisfying conclusion to the story.

Simplified story structure 3: The hero's journey

This structure was popularized by Joseph Campbell in *The Hero with a Thousand Faces*, which explains ancient mythological stories through the lens of the hero.

There are seventeen detailed steps, but they can be grouped in three main stages.

> **Departure:** The hero lives in an ordinary world and receives a call to adventure. The hero refuses the call and resists the adventure but,

with the help of a mentor figure, decides to go on a quest.

Initiation: The hero faces a series of tasks and challenges, has to fight battles, finds allies and enemies, and learns things along the way. In the climax, the hero must overcome their biggest challenge and find what they seek.

Return: The hero returns to the real world changed and with important lessons to share.

The hero is not necessarily male. The structure is more about one central character and follows their arc, while side characters are less important. The hero must improve their skill and defeat an enemy alone. The climax may even be a one-on-one battle.

Classic examples of the hero's journey in film include *Star Wars, The Matrix, Wonder Woman*, and characters like James Bond and Lara Croft. In terms of books, Lee Child's Jack Reacher is a classic hero, and my ARKANE series has a classic hero in Morgan Sierra, who I modeled partly on Lara Croft.

Simplified story structure 4: The heroine's journey

The heroine's journey is not just a female version of the hero's journey. As Gail Carriger explains in *The Heroine's Journey*, "Biological sex characteristics are irrelevant to whether a main character is a hero or a heroine."

The heroine's journey is more about "networking, connecting with others, and finding family." Side characters are important, and the story is all about the team, the companions, working together, and strengthening relationships in order to overcome obstacles. The end goal is to be happy, surrounded by family and friends.

Carriger uses Harry Potter as an example of a heroine in her book, arguing that the books "more than anything else, are about the sensation of *belonging*," and "his success is nested in the networks he forms and the friendships he makes… Harry has friends and he is not alone."

While the basic story structure might be similar to the hero's journey, the characters and the plot will be different, as it's essentially about community over the individual.

Can you reject all forms of structure and do something original?

Of course, you can write whatever you like in whatever way you like.

In 2019, Lucy Ellmann won the £10,000 Goldsmiths Prize, given for 'fiction at its most novel,' with *Ducks, Newburyport*, which is one long sentence of internal monologue continuing for over 1,000 pages. As reported in the *Guardian*, Ellmann said of her work, "I sense people are hungry for something new, and sick of fiction that lazily kowtows to the reader or, God help us, the 'market.'"

Your answer to this question comes down to what kind of reader you are as well as what kind of writer. I love escaping into thrillers, dark fantasy, and horror. I love explosive action-adventure movies. I *am* 'the reader' and 'the market,' so I write the books I want to read.

You must do the same.

Will story structure make your writing unoriginal and cliché?

> "When forced to work within a strict framework, the imagination is taxed to its utmost and will produce its richest ideas. Given total freedom, the work is likely to sprawl."
>
> —*T.S. Eliot*

The simplified story structures above can be laid over pretty much every story in existence for every genre in every age.

Your story does not need an original structure. It needs original characters and plot and setting and detail and theme — and all the things that only you can bring to it.

You can be more creative within boundaries, so take a simple structure and use it to make sure your story satisfies readers, whatever the genre.

Questions:

- Which story structure/s might work best for your idea?
- Which story structures do you want to learn more about? How will you prevent yourself from drowning in analysis?
- How will you use structure while also bringing originality to your writing?

Resources:

- *Anatomy of Story: 22 Steps to Becoming a Master Storyteller* — John Truby
- *Romancing the Beat: Story Structure for Romance Novels* — Gwen Hayes
- *Save the Cat! Writes a Novel: The Last Book on Novel Writing You'll Ever Need* — Jessica Brody
- *Story: Substance, Structure, Style, and The Principles of Screenwriting* — Robert McKee
- *Take Off Your Pants! Outline Your Books for Faster, Better Writing* — Libbie Hawker
- *The Heroine's Journey: For Writers, Readers, and Fans of Pop Culture* — Gail Carriger

- *The Story Grid: What Good Editors Know* — Shawn Coyne

- *The Writer's Journey: Mythic Structure for Writers* — Christopher Vogler

- Interview with Gail Carriger on the heroine's journey — www.TheCreativePenn.com/heroines-journey

- "One long sentence, 1,000 pages: Lucy Ellmann 'masterpiece' wins Goldsmiths prize," *The Guardian*, 13 November, 2019 — www.theguardian.com/books/2019/nov/13/eight-sentences-over-1000-pages-lucy-ellmann-masterpiece-wins-goldsmiths-prize

3.2 Scenes and chapters

When you read a book, you experience the story through chapters that the author has organized to guide you through the book in a linear fashion.

But you don't have to write that way.

In fact, most authors write in scenes and structure them into chapters later.

Learning about scenes was a pivotal moment in my writing journey. It freed me up creatively because I realized I could just write intuitively and structure later.

It also gives me a concrete goal to focus on during writing sessions. I aim to write a scene, rather than a specific number of words. I mostly write out of order, writing scenes as they come up in my mind, following story threads regardless of where they might end up in the finished book. After I've written the whole story in scenes, I organize them into chapters.

What is a chapter? What is a scene?

A chapter is a sub-division of a book, often numbered or sometimes with short descriptors about character or plot elements.

A scene has a character, or characters, in a setting performing some kind of action toward a specific goal.

The intention of a scene is to advance the story, reveal aspects of character, or explore theme at a deeper level.

There can be multiple scenes in a chapter, usually separated by three asterisks or an ornamental break. The change of scene might represent a shift in point of view, or a time jump, or a setting change.

You can also split a scene across chapters, which can make readers want to turn the page, desperate to know what's coming next. These cliff-hangers can improve pacing and tension.

For some authors, one scene equals one chapter. James Patterson's novels often have hundreds of short chapters, all of which are one scene. Other authors have multiple scenes within a smaller number of chapters.

"If a scene doesn't work, nothing else matters. You can create a brilliant premise, but if you can't nail the execution, the reader will not turn the page."

—J. Thorn, *Three Story Method: Writing Scenes*

How a scene works

My thriller *Crypt of Bone* opens with an Israeli soldier walking in the dawn light toward the Western Wall in Jerusalem, ready to begin his guard shift.

As he prays at the wall, he hears a shout from high on the plaza above. If you don't know Jerusalem, the Dome of the Rock, sacred to Muslims, sits above the Western Wall, sacred to Jews. It's a highly contested religious site and a flash point for violence.

The soldier pulls his rifle out, ready for trouble, but sees only a man in a white hospital gown standing above. The man jumps and smashes onto the stones below, his blood staining the sanctuary. He clutches a slip of paper in his hand with the sketch of a pale horse's head and a quote from the book of Revelation, *"Before me was a pale horse. Its rider was named Death, and Hades followed close behind."*

In this scene, the setting is the Western Wall in Jerusalem, and the character is the Israeli soldier, Ayal

Ben-David. The scene is written from Ayal's point of view (POV). He is Jewish, so the reader understands how important this place is from a religious and spiritual angle, and the location underscores the theme and tone of the story, which is a religious conspiracy thriller.

The scene has action. Ayal walks in the streets before praying at the wall, then witnesses the suicide, and finally picks up the scrap of paper and reads the prophecy.

The scene moves the story forward and opens questions in the reader's mind: Who is the dead man? Why did he jump? Why was he holding the apocalyptic lines about the pale horse — and what else might be coming with Death and Hades?

If I had written the scene from the POV of the man who jumps from the wall, readers would know the answers to these questions and there would be no mystery.

Make sure there's a value shift across the scene

The value shift relates to some kind of change. Without a change, a scene can feel slow and static.

In the previous example, Ayal starts his day, walking to pray in the dawn before his guard shift — a positive moment.

Then he witnesses a suicide, his holy sanctuary is stained with blood, and he reads an apocalyptic prophecy that threatens the status quo — a negative moment.

The Story Grid by Shawn Coyne explores this idea of story value in more detail, giving examples of different kinds, including internal changes.

Break the scene across chapters to create a cliff-hanger

> "A book you simply cannot put down —
> this being your goal — is a book with great scenes
> that propel you toward other great scenes."
>
> —Larry Brooks, *Story Engineering*

If you want to keep the reader turning the pages, then break your scenes across chapters.

Choose a point where you have opened a loop in the reader's mind that they must close, then cut to another scene.

Here's an example from *Blood Infernal* by James Rollins and Rebecca Cantrell, a fantastic supernatural thriller.

"A dark figure snaked out of the darkness and into the light. Jordan barely registered the fangs before it launched straight at him."

That's the end of the chapter. Of course you want to turn the page and read the next one!

But the next chapter is a scene featuring another character, and the story doesn't return to Jordan for another two and a half chapters. If you are strategic with cutting and organizing scenes, you can create multiple cliff-hangers from multiple POV characters, so the reader is pulled through the pages with multiple nesting open loops. A new cliff-hanger is presented by the time the previous one is resolved.

Here's another example from *Honeymoon* by James Patterson: "Then Nora heard something — footsteps approaching the kitchen. *Someone else was in the house.*"

End of chapter.

You don't have to write such dramatic cliff-hangers, of course. It will depend on the genre and the kind of loop you want to open in the reader's mind.

Remember, the chapter is the organizational unit of the novel, so you can restructure your scenes into chapters in the editing process.

How long is a scene? How long is a chapter?

This is a personal choice and can become part of an author's style. James Patterson has 117 chapters in his novel *Honeymoon*, which is about 75,000 words. That's only 641 words on average per short, pacey chapter. Some chapters are only one page.

The Shining by Stephen King is over 100,000 words and only has 57 chapters.

As ever, it's up to you.

But however long they are, write in scenes, organize into chapters later.

Pacing

A reader experiences your story in a linear way. They start at the beginning and (hopefully) read or listen to the end. Your job as a writer is to control how they proceed through the story, and pacing is one aspect that can affect their experience.

Pacing varies by genre. For example, fans of thrillers expect more action scenes than fans of cozy mysteries, and the literary reader may prefer long paragraphs of introspection rather than choppy scenes with a lot of dialogue.

You can speed up reading pace with your writing style.

Hit the return key.

So there are shorter lines on the page.

More lines on the page.

More white space.

Just like this.

Your eyes will move faster down the written page, and the audiobook narration will similarly sound more pacey.

You can achieve this with dialogue pinging back and forth between characters, which is faster to read. You can also use dashes and other punctuation.

Examine a James Patterson novel in ebook or print so you can see how much white space he uses during scenes. That white space, along with his short chapters, keep the reader turning the page.

You can lengthen a scene by writing longer sentences, which can run into longer paragraphs. Spend more time on setting descriptions or the point-of-view character's thoughts and emotions about the situation, so you linger in the story. The prose will look denser on the page in a story with a slower pace.

Make sure you have a balance of scenes. If you have a fast-paced scene, consider adding a slower scene next, perhaps featuring a subplot, so the reader can take a breath before you speed things up again. You can even balance pacing within scenes.

You will get a sense for it over time. It just takes practice.

Questions:

- How long is a typical scene in your genre? How long is a chapter? Check your example books and see what the authors do, but don't let them constrain you.
- How long do you expect your chapters and scenes to be?
- Are there a few scenes in your novel you can already clearly visualize? Could writing these

scenes first, even if they are out of order, help you get started?

- What are some natural places in your story where you could create cliff-hangers using scene and chapter breaks? Find examples from your favorite books.

- What kind of pacing is typical in your genre? Which techniques for controlling pacing will work well for your novel?

Resources:

- *Story Engineering: Mastering the 6 Core Competencies of Successful Writing* — Larry Brooks

- *The Story Grid: What Good Editors Know* — Shawn Coyne

- *Three Story Method: Writing Scenes* — J. Thorn

3.3 Character: Who is the story about?

> "People are more interested in people than anything else."
>
> —*Bob Mayer, The Novel Writer's Toolkit*

Characters are the heart of fiction. If you consider any memorable book, film, or TV series, it will often be the characters you remember most, along with the feelings or emotional resonances you experienced along the way.

You need all kinds of characters in your story, but how you create them and when they emerge in your writing process is up to you.

Some writers produce reams of character notes before they start, including details, from favorite color to how they got the scar on their lower back, that may not even appear in the book.

Others start with plot or theme or setting and create a character to fit the story later.

You can't tell from a finished novel which way the writer created their characters, and there is no one correct way to go about it, but there are some fundamentals to consider.

Who are the different characters in your story?

Your **protagonist** is the main character and is introduced at the beginning or at least early in the book, so the reader knows who they are and understands their significance.

They are usually interesting in some way, or might have special skills, or if they are a 'normal' person, they develop into something more that makes them special during the book.

Much of the book will be written from their point of view (a topic covered in more detail in the next chapter) so choose or create your protagonist based on the most interesting perspective for your story.

You can have multiple protagonists, but this can complicate the story considerably. If this is your first novel, consider using a single protagonist, which will make the book easier to write and finish. *The Hunger Games* is a great example of a successful novel with a single protagonist. There are other characters, but Katniss Everdeen is the clear protagonist.

Your **antagonist** is the character who tries to stop the protagonist from getting what they want, and they need a believable motivation for their actions and approach. The antagonist doesn't have to be a person, however. In the classic '90s disaster movie *Armageddon*, the primary antagonist is the asteroid that will destroy Earth.

You also need **secondary characters**, and these will depend on the needs of your story and your genre. There might be a sidekick, a mentor, a love interest, a team of some kind, or a friendship group.

You need a bigger cast of characters if you want to kill off some of them along the way. *A Game of Thrones* is a great example of this.

You might also want to spin off secondary characters into their own books, where they are the protagonist. Romance authors do this really well. In the Bridgerton books and TV show, each of the siblings is the protagonist of their specific story, and a secondary character in the other books. This strategy keeps readers hooked into wanting to know what happens to them all.

Readers must want to spend time with the character/s

If you write characters that readers care about or are interested in, they will forgive a lot of other things about the story.

The characters don't have to be lovable or even likable — that will depend on your genre and story choices — but they have to be captivating enough that we want to spend time with them by reading the story.

A great example is the TV show *Succession*, which is about a billionaire media mogul and his family. There are no likable characters, but it is utterly compelling to watch them self-destruct.

Characters that span series can deepen the reader's relationship with them as you expand their back story and relationships into new plots. Readers will remember the character more than the plot or the book title and look forward to (and hopefully pre-order) the next in series because they want more time with your characters. British crime author Angela Marsons said in an interview that her readers experience returning to her characters as like "putting on a pair of old slippers."

Character description and character tags

> "Fiction is about the particular, not the generic and 'ordinary.'"
>
> —*Roz Morris, Nail Your Novel: Writing Characters Who'll Keep Readers Captivated*

Some writers like to imagine which actors they'd cast in their character roles to bring them alive. I find pictures of actors and paste them into my Scrivener project. This helps with visuals but also with the sense of the character.

My ARKANE agent Morgan Sierra has always been Angelina Jolie in *Lara Croft* or *Mr and Mrs Smith*, and Blake Daniel in my Brooke and Daniel crime thriller series was based on Jesse Williams, best known as Dr Jackson Avery in *Grey's Anatomy*.

You need specific details about the characters to make them seem real.

Consider using character tags, little details that anchor them in the reader's mind. Robert Galbraith's Cormoran Strike is an amputee, and his pain and the physical challenges of his prosthesis are a key part of every story.

My character Blake Daniel always wears gloves to cover the scars on his hands, which provides an angle into his wounded past as well as a visual cue for the reader.

A character tag might also be a specific kind of dialogue or action that contrasts with how others speak or behave and can be used by a group of characters. *A Game of Thrones* by George R.R. Martin features different family houses with various mottos and sigils. The Starks say "Winter is coming," and their sigil is a dire wolf.

Character flaws and wounds

Everyone has issues.

It's true in real life, and it's even more true in fiction. Your characters cannot be happy and perfect in every way — unless that is a feature of the story itself.

Character flaws are aspects of personality that affect the person so much that it is a challenge to face and overcome them. These character flaws can become central to the plot. In *Jaws* by Peter Benchley, the protagonist Brody is afraid of the water, but he has to overcome that flaw to destroy the killer shark and save the town.

You can imagine a flaw for almost any aspect of a character. Choose a flaw that will create the effects you need for your character and plot. Some flaws are about personality. A character who values status above all else might choose to marry for money, but perhaps they can only find true love when they overcome that flaw.

Some flaws are more life-threatening. For example, a character with an addiction to painkillers might lie to cover up spending patterns and spiral into debt in order to fund their need.

Remember, your characters should feel like real people, so never define them purely by their flaws. The character addicted to painkillers might also be a brilliant and successful female lawyer who gets up at four o'clock in the morning to work out at the gym, likes '80s music, and volunteers at the local dog shelter at the weekends. There are plenty of functional addicts who don't fit the stereotype too often seen in the media. Part of your job as a writer is to break out of cliché and write original, compelling characters.

Character wounds are formed from life experience and are part of your character's backstory. These are often traumatic events that happened before the events of your novel, but they shape the character's reactions in the present story.

In my ARKANE thrillers, Morgan Sierra's husband Elian died in her arms during a military operation. This happened before the series begins, but her memories of it recur when she faces a firefight, and she struggles to find happiness again for fear of losing someone she loves once more.

Trauma affects people differently, so don't assume certain reactions. For example, the COVID-19 pandemic has been traumatic for so many, but its impact on behavior varies. For some, hand-washing and virus-avoidance practices have turned into Obsessive Compulsive Disorder (OCD). Others don't want to leave the safety of their home ever again. Some have scarred lungs, others have scarred memories. Still others can't wait to get back out in the world and seek adventure once more.

Question your initial assumptions about what a wound might be and how it affects your character. For more ideas, check out *The Emotional Wound Thesaurus: A Writer's Guide to Psychological Trauma* by Becca Puglisi and Angela Ackerman.

Character emotion

"We're wired to crave, hunt for, and latch on to what the protagonist feels so that we can experience his struggles as if they were our own."

—Lisa Cron, *Story Genius*

One reason we read is to get inside the heads of other people. We want to know how they feel as they go through the events of the story. We want to be moved. We want to close the book with a sigh of satisfaction.

You can achieve this with your story if you write your characters with enough depth to evoke emotion in the reader. Take them into the mind and experience of the character by using sensory details about the setting and the character's emotional reaction to what happens.

Someone with a phobia of snakes might have a physical reaction to seeing one — sweating palms, raised heart rate, narrowed vision, churning stomach. They might feel a need to run away or curl up like a child and weep, or they might take drugs to numb themselves if they have no choice but to face their fear. They might remember the events that caused the phobia in the first place, regret how it impacts their life now, or swear to get therapy so they are not so out of control next time.

Check out *The Emotion Thesaurus: A Writer's Guide to Character Expression* by Becca Puglisi and Angela Ackerman for help writing emotion.

Show, don't tell

> "When a writer tells, they have made the judgement for the reader. When a writer shows, they offer the evidence and let the reader decide that the character is fun, talented, beautiful, mean, cruel, generous, or troubled. The reader owns the judgment and remembers it because they made it themselves. Which is exactly how we form conclusions about flesh-and-blood people."
>
> —Roz Morris, *Nail Your Novel: Writing Characters Who'll Keep Readers Captivated*

Most writers have heard the saying 'show, don't tell' so many times that it's easy to nod and say, 'yes, I must do that,' and then promptly write scenes that tell rather than show.

It's simple to say, but it takes practice. It's harder than it sounds.

Basically, you need to reveal your character through action and dialogue, rather than explanation.

In my thriller *Day of the Vikings*, ARKANE agent Morgan Sierra fights a Neo-Viking in the halls of the British Museum and brings down a man bigger than she is with her Krav Maga martial art ability, which she learned and honed in the Israeli military.

Telling would be something like, "Morgan was an expert in Krav Maga and she easily brought down the Neo-Viking."

Showing is a longer, more active fight scene that demonstrates Morgan's capabilities and the edge of her anger, which she barely keeps in control. In the previous scene, she had introduced herself as an academic, and now the reader sees she is definitely more than that. The fight scene is not just about showing action. It also opens up questions about her back story, demonstrates aspects of character, and moves the plot forward.

Telling has its place, of course, but make sure you are using it only when you need it — for example, when summarizing a past event. You can correct too much telling in your edits if the balance is off in the first draft.

Character names

Your main character names are important, especially if you are creating a series character who lives on across multiple books.

Some character names will come to you and seem 'right' in some way. At least this happens to me in the discovery writing process. The names Morgan Sierra and Jamie Brooke, both strong female protagonists and the leads of two of my series, came to me clearly as I thought about the stories I wanted to tell.

For secondary characters, once I know their nationality and age, I google actors and use a combination of names. For Asha Kapoor, the Indian antagonist in *Destroyer of Worlds*, I googled 'young Indian Hindu actress' and then chose from a combination of names that came up. Hindu names are different from Muslim or Christian names, so if religion is important, make sure you account for that.

You can also use baby name sites to look up meanings and ancestral links to underscore aspects of character. In *Map of Shadows*, I picked Sienna's surname, Farren, because it means adventurous.

A name can also have deeper resonance. One example is a secondary character, Corium Jones, in my crime thriller, *Deviance*. The word *corium* is Latin for *dermis*, a skin layer, and also the thickened, leathery part of an insect forewing. The character Corium preserves human skin covered in tattoos, so his name is an important aspect of the character and underscores the theme of the novel.

Make sure you google the name of the character to check if there is a public figure with similarities to your fictional character. Your character name doesn't have to be original, but you don't want to mistakenly use someone real in a recognizable way. For *One Day in Budapest*, I created a Hungarian right-wing politician using my actor technique and then discovered that there was, in fact, a politician by that name in Hungary. I changed my character's name!

Once you've chosen a name, read it out loud so you know how it will sound in the reader's head and also in the audio version of your book. You will default to certain names, so at some point in the process, make a list of all your characters in alphabetical order to ensure you have variety in the letters they start with and in the sound of their names.

Names are also important as they signal to the reader that this character is worth paying attention to. Don't name a character if they are just a 'walk on' — for example, a waiter who brings a drink to your character in a bar. You don't need to name the waiter unless they play a more significant role.

Character archetypes

You should aim to create original characters, but you can use archetypes as a way to underscore their role and purpose in the story. Examples of archetypes include the Mentor, the Ally, and the Magician.

These roles appear in ancient stories and myths and have been expanded into psychological archetypes by the psychologist Carl Jung, and further by Joseph Campbell in *The Hero with a Thousand Faces*.

You can easily spot archetypes in books and movies. I love the character of Q in the James Bond movies. He represents a Geek or Nerd archetype, solving technological questions, introducing cool gadgets, and helping Bond with the more intellectual side of cases. I created Martin Klein, my geeky ARKANE archivist, in that archetypal role and, over the series, he has developed into so much more. Through him, I explore my fascination with artificial intelligence, and how technology overlaps with aspects of religion. I even have ideas for stand-alone stories with Martin as I identify with him so much.

What do your characters want?

What does your protagonist want? Why do they want it? Is there an external reason and/or an internal reason for wanting it?

This desire may be on multiple levels. For example, Phil joins the military at a time of war. She wants to serve her country. She also wants to get out of her dead-end town and do something with her life. This way, she can earn a living and learn new skills, and maybe even travel. The risk is worth it.

But maybe her motivation goes deeper.

Phil's father and grandfather served in the military and, by joining up, she will finally earn their respect and maybe even love after years of being ignored as the only girl in the family. Perhaps she has never found real friends in her small town, but in the military, she will be accepted into a community and find her place in the world. This could turn into a coming-of-age story, or maybe a romance.

Or perhaps Phil's father died on a military mission under mysterious circumstances, and she wants to find out what happened from the inside. This could become a mystery or a thriller, because her true desire is to find out the truth and avenge her father.

Consider layers of motivation in your story. What a character really wants deep down will be more complex than just the surface desire.

Who or what is trying to stop your character getting what they want?

Your antagonist also wants something, often diametrically opposed to your protagonist. They also need a good reason for it, or at least a reason that makes sense to them.

In my ARKANE thriller *Tree of Life*, Aurelia dos Santos Fidalgo is the heiress of a Brazilian mining empire. She wants to restore the Earth to its original state to atone for the destruction caused by her father's company, and she is part of a radical ecological group who believe that the only way to restore Nature is to end all human life. This is a believable motivation in an era of climate change, but clearly Morgan and Jake have to stop her.

Once you understand who or what the antagonist is and what they want, you will get ideas for the conflicts and challenges that will fuel the plot.

Back story

Apart from the very occasional exception, most fictional stories don't start with the birth of a character and then share every detail of the character's life over the course of the book. The story begins with an inciting incident, something that interrupts the character's status quo. There will always be back story: the stuff that happened before this story started.

You don't need to describe it all, and readers don't need to know everything about the character in chapter one.

When we meet people for the first time, or the second, or the third, we might only glimpse their past and discover the occasional detail about them over time. Even when we have known someone for many years, we never know everything about their lives. In the same way, you do not need to share your character's entire history at the beginning of your novel, or in fact, ever. Share whatever is needed to serve the story as it becomes necessary.

This also ties into 'show, don't tell.' In my ARKANE thrillers, I don't need to tell you about Morgan's military history straight away. I can wait until there's a fight scene, then demonstrate her competency, and then have her internal thoughts reflect on the past.

Character arc

How does your character change through the course of the story?

They will inevitably grow and change because of the events that happen and the decisions they make. You can reveal the progression of character through action, dialogue, and internal thought.

The arc is more easily demonstrated if you make the character's position more obvious at the beginning because the shift happens over the course of the story, and it is clear where the character must end up.

In my dark fantasy thriller *Risen Gods*, co-written with J. Thorn, Ben Henare rejects his Maori heritage and its associated mythology. By the end of the book, he has to embrace it in order to defeat the risen gods who threaten Aotearoa New Zealand. Along the way, Ben must face supernatural creatures he previously didn't believe to exist.

Different stories suit different character arcs, and if you're writing a series, then the character can't change dramatically every time. Lee Child's Jack Reacher is a Lone Ranger type of character. In every novel, he arrives in a town alone, dispenses justice, defends the weak, kills the bad guys, and then leaves — alone once more. He is essentially unchanged by his experience, except for a few more bruises.

In contrast, literary fiction novels primarily focus on character arc with less emphasis on plot. You can choose how extreme your character arc becomes in your story.

Using people you know as the basis for character

Our life experiences and the people we meet along the way inevitably end up woven into our stories somehow, but beware of creating characters that are exactly like people you know. Use composites instead. Take aspects of real people and combine them with others to create unique characters.

My ARKANE series protagonist Morgan Sierra is definitely my alter ego, and her musings on religion and the supernatural are often my own. But her Krav Maga fighting skill and her ability to kill the bad guys are definitely her own!

Write diverse characters

The world is a diverse place, so your fiction needs to be populated with all kinds of people.

If I only populated my fiction with characters like me, they would be boring novels indeed!

There are many dimensions of difference. Race, nationality, sex, age, body type, ability, religion, gender, sexual orientation, socio-economic status, class, culture, education level, job, values, and so much more.

All these shape character worldview and, even then, don't assume that similar types of people think the same, regardless of their shared experiences.

When the UK split over the Brexit vote, many were surprised by people who voted a certain way against expectations. Similarly, behavior and opinions during the pandemic often didn't conform to type. Part of your job as a writer is to bring believable characters to life, and humans are truly diverse. Don't box a character in. Consider different aspects of their lives rather than just what's on the surface.

Some authors worry they will make mistakes when writing diverse characters. We live in a time of outrage, and many authors have been criticized for writing outside their own experience. A few have even been 'cancelled' for their opinions.

So, is it just too dangerous to write diverse characters?

Of course not.

The media amplifies outliers, and most authors include diverse characters in every book without causing offense because they work hard to get it right.

It's about awareness, research, and intent.

To start, be aware of how diverse your characters are. Have you written a mono-cultural perspective for all of them? Is that an accurate representation of the world of your story? Either design the book to contain different people or go back through and diversify your cast in the editing phase.

Then research. Don't write what you know. Write what you want to learn about.

I love research. It's part of why I'm an author in the first place. I take any excuse to dive into a world different from my own!

I write international thrillers and dark fantasy, and my fiction is populated with characters from all over the world. I have a multi-cultural family and I have lived in many places and traveled widely, so I have met, worked with, and had relationships with people from different cultures. I find story ideas through travel and if I set my books in a certain place, then, of course, the story is populated with the people who live there.

Destroyer of Worlds is set mostly in India, a country I love and have traveled in several times. As part of my research, I read books about Hindu myth and watched documentaries about the *sadhus*, the holy men. One of my Indian readers from Mumbai also read the story to check my cultural references.

Risen Gods is a dark fantasy YA story set in New Zealand with a young Maori man, Ben, and a white Pakeha woman, Lucy. A tsunami separates the friends and they travel the length of the country, fighting mythical creatures as the volcanoes erupt and the Maori gods rise again. I am a New Zealand citizen and lived there for several years. My husband is a Kiwi and we still have family there. I studied books about Maori mythology and fiction written by Maori authors. One of my male Maori readers read the story to check for cultural issues, and a vulcanologist read for accuracy on eruptions.

The opening scene of ARKANE thriller *End of Days* is set in an Appalachian snake-handling church in the USA. I transcribed hours of video from such churches on YouTube to try and understand the worldview of the worshippers, as my antagonist, Lilith, was brought up in that tradition.

Research using books, films, and podcasts, and focus particularly on those produced by people from the worldview you want to learn about. You can often find readers in your community or hire sensitivity readers if you want to be certain you have done a decent job. (See chapter 5.4 for more detail.)

It's also about intent.

Readers are smart, and they will perceive an author's intent from the book. My sister-in-law is Nigerian, and we were sitting together once with some other people having a drink. One person said something that I thought she might be offended by. While the content was questionable, she noted that they did not intend to offend. It was easy to tell the difference. The comment came from a place of ignorance, not an intent to harm.

Do your research. Try your best. Ask for help to get it right. Apologize if you need to. But, please, write diverse characters.

Check out *Writing the Other: A Practical Approach* by Nisi Shawl and Cynthia Ward, and their website WritingTheOther.com for more help in getting this right.

Questions:

- Make a list of characters from books, movies or TV shows you love. What makes them memorable, interesting, or compelling?

- Who are the different characters in your story? If you know them already, then you can start to make notes about them. If you don't know yet, don't worry, you can create them along the way.

- Why will readers want to spend time with these characters?

- How can you use specific character description and tags to bring them alive? Add these details to your character notes if you have a list already.

- What flaws and wounds might your characters have that add depth and potential to your story? Have you made sure your characters are fully realized, and not purely defined by one thing?

- What are the primary emotions your protagonist will experience over the course of the novel? How can you deepen those emotions and show them on the page?

- What does 'show, don't tell' mean in practice for your novel? For your story, which aspects are most important to show?

- What resources will you use to choose character names?

- How could you use character archetypes to enrich your characters?

- What does your protagonist want? Why do they want it? Can you go deeper into their motivations?

- Who or what is trying to stop your character from getting what they want? What is the antagonist's believable motivation?

- What part does back story play in your story? How much do readers need to know, and how can you weave it into the novel rather than delivering it as an info dump?

- Does your character have an arc in the novel? How do they grow and change?

- How will you integrate aspects of people you know into characters?
- Does your novel include diverse characters? If not, how can you revise your cast of characters to make it more diverse? What resources will you draw on to make sure your representations are accurate and believable?

Resources:

- *Creating Character Arcs: The Masterful Author's Guide to Uniting Story Structure, Plot, and Character Development*
— K.M. Weiland

- *Nail Your Novel: Writing Characters Who'll Keep Readers Captivated* — Roz Morris

- *The Emotion Thesaurus: A Writer's Guide to Character Expression* — Angela Ackerman and Becca Puglisi

- *The Emotional Wound Thesaurus: A Writer's Guide to Psychological Trauma*
— Becca Puglisi and Angela Ackerman

- *The Hero with a Thousand Faces*
— Joseph Campbell

- *The Heroine with 1001 Faces* — Maria Tatar
- *The Novel Writer's Toolkit: From Idea to Bestseller* — Bob Mayer
- *The Science of Storytelling: Why Stories Make Us Human and How To Tell Them Better* — Will Storr
- *Wired for Story: The Writer's Guide to Using Brain Science to Hook Readers from the Very First Sentence* — Lisa Cron
- *Writing the Other: A Practical Approach* — Nisi Shawl and Cynthia Ward
- Website with resources and classes on writing diverse characters: www.WritingTheOther.com
- Interview with Angela Marsons on writing a successful crime thriller series on The Creative Penn Podcast, May 2022 — www.TheCreativePenn.com/angelamarsons

3.4 Point of view

Point of view (POV) is about the particular perspective you tell your story from and which character or characters you choose to focus on for your book. This choice shapes the language of your novel.

But your choice of POV also affects story structure, plot, and the reader's experience. You need to choose the right POV to tell the right story, and some writers will start one way and shift later because they find more creative gold writing from another character's POV.

How does POV change the story?

Take your life as an example. Here's an example from mine.

I'm the eldest of five siblings and I am twelve years older than my youngest sister. My parents divorced when I was young. I'm happily married for the second time, but my first marriage and divorce were difficult.

Here are some different story angles based on POV:

- My divorce story from my POV.

- The divorce story told from my ex-husband's POV. Very different from my own!
- A family wedding story with scenes from my youngest sister's POV as well as my dad's POV, and perhaps the celebrant's as well. Different generations, unique life experiences, and varied views on marriage and love.

Think about the story you want to tell. How might it change if you choose to write from the perspective of a different character?

Let's look at the most popular POVs to help you decide.

First-person POV: I walked into the bar.

The use of 'I' demonstrates first-person POV. The scene is told from that character's perspective and the reader is in their head. It is intimate and readers often feel a deep connection to the character this way.

Narrating an entire book from first-person POV can limit your story. The character can only be in one place at one time. The reader has to stay with that character and can't know any more than the character knows.

Some authors do use multiple first person POVs, but that can be confusing for the reader — and the author!

First person POV is more common in particular genres, including YA (young adult) and romance.

From *The Hunger Games* by Suzanne Collins:

> When I wake up, the other side of the bed is cold. My fingers stretch out, seeking Prim's warmth but finding only the rough canvas cover of the mattress. She must have had bad dreams and climbed in with our mother. Of course she did. This is the day of the reaping.

From *Fifty Shades of Grey* by E.L. James:

> I scowl with frustration at myself in the mirror. Damn my hair — it just won't behave, and damn Katherine Kavanagh for being ill and subjecting me to this ordeal. I should be studying for my final exams, which are next week, yet here I am trying to brush my hair into submission.

Third person POV: Jim walked into the bar.

This is most commonly used in novels because you can tell the story from multiple different perspectives.

George R.R. Martin does this in *A Game of Thrones*, telling the story from different character viewpoints in third-person POV. He even titles his chapters with the character names, which helps readers get oriented right away, though alternatively you can just use the character's name in the first sentence of the chapter.

For example, here is the first sentence of the first chapter from Jon Snow's POV:

> There were times — not many, but a few — when Jon Snow was glad he was a bastard. As he filled his wine cup once more from a passing flagon, it struck him that this might be one of them.

If you need to expand a book, just add more character POV chapters.

But beware, *A Game of Thrones* is also a good example of how a book or series will expand considerably if you add more POV characters. If you have to write the entire story from the POV of five major characters, all of whom have well-defined character arcs, then you may end up with a series as long and sprawling as Martin's.

Most stories have one main protagonist and the chapters of the book are weighted toward their POV, interspersed with POV chapters from minor characters as needed to move the plot forward.

I predominantly write my ARKANE thrillers from Morgan Sierra's POV with a few scenes from the antagonist and also from Jake, Morgan's ARKANE agent partner, and sometimes others. When I wanted to explore Jake further as a character, I wrote him a whole separate story in *One Day in New York*.

Third-person limited or close third-person POV is when you only see the story from the character's perspective. Third-person omniscient can give a more bird's eye view of the scene but if you're not careful, you can end up head-hopping (more on that below!).

Second person POV: You walk into the bar.

This is rarely used for a whole book as it's difficult to write and difficult to read, although some authors use it effectively for a chapter.

Here's an example from *How to Get Filthy Rich in Rising Asia* by Mohsin Hamid:

> The whites of your eyes are yellow, a consequence of spiking bilirubin levels in your blood. The virus afflicting you is called hepatitis E. Its typical mode of transmission is fecal-oral. Yum. It kills only about one in fifty, so you're likely to recover. But right now you feel like you're going to die.

Can you blend different POVs in one story?

Yes. You can have some chapters that are first person, others that are third person, or whatever combination you like.

Thriller author Lisa Gardner uses such a combination in *Catch Me*.

From the Prologue in third person:

> The little girl woke up the way she'd been trained: quickly and quietly. She inhaled once, a hushed gasp in the still night, then her eyes fixed on her mother's drawn face.

From Chapter 1 in first person:

> My name is Charlene Rosalind Carter Grant. I live in Boston, work in Boston, and in four days, will probably die here. I'm twenty-eight years old. And I don't feel like dying just yet.

From Chapter 2 in third person, but a different character from the Prologue:

> Boston sergeant detective D. D. Warren was on the case and she was not happy about it.

The rhythm of alternating POVs is maintained through the book, blending intimacy with a wider perspective.

What tense will work for your book?

Most writers will have a default tense they prefer to write in, and any of these POVs could be written in past tense or present tense.

If you're telling the story in real time, you can use present tense. It's immediate. The reader feels like they are right there in the moment, experiencing the story with the character.

If you're telling it as a narrator about the past, it's a memory so can be past tense. Past tense, like third person, is more flexible. It's easier to weave in back story and interior thoughts because the narrator has had more time for reflection.

Again, you can blend tenses across a book, but it's not often done within a chapter or scene. Revisit the books you love and see how they use tense.

Beware 'head-hopping' within a scene

If you're writing from a particular character's POV within a scene, stay with that character. Don't 'head-hop' into another perspective. Make it very clear whose perspective you're in for each scene.

This is a common issue with new writers, and although there are always exceptions, you will generally find that even the most rule-breaking writers stick to this one.

If you want to write from another character's perspective, consider using a different chapter, as Gardner and Martin do in the earlier examples. Or use an ornamental break in the text to indicate a switch within a scene.

How to decide what POV to write in

Revisit the five to ten books that are like the story you're writing, or any of your favorite novels. What POV are they written in? Does it vary by scene or chapter?

Some authors have a natural sense of how they want to write, and if the majority of the books you love are written in a particular POV, then that's probably the one to write in.

Personally, I like to read and write in third person. I want chapters from the antagonist as well as the protagonist. I want a chapter from someone who ends up dying later. First-person novels are too restrictive for me. But then I know lots of authors who love reading and writing in first person, and I occasionally write this way for short stories.

Only you can decide for your novel — and of course, you can always change it as you write.

It's all too complicated!

Don't spend too long deliberating on POV and tense. Start writing and you will probably find yourself using aspects naturally without overthinking it. You can always clean it up in the editing phase, and if you work with a professional editor, they can help you, too.

Questions:

- Think about the story you want to tell. How might it change if you choose to write from the perspective of different characters?

- Revisit the five to ten books that are like the story you're writing, or just any of your favorite novels. What POV are they written in? Does it vary by scene or chapter?

- What POV will you write in? What tense will you write in? If you can't decide, just start writing and your preference will probably emerge.

Resources:

- *Point of View: How to use the different POV types, avoid head-hopping, and choose the best point of view for your book* — Sandra Gerth

- *Steering The Craft: A Twenty-First Century Guide to Sailing the Sea of Story*
  — Ursula K. Le Guin

3.5 Dialogue

"Writing good dialogue is art as well as craft."

—*Stephen King, On Writing*

Dialogue is how characters communicate with each other. As your characters speak, they reveal aspects of their attitudes and back story, and when they talk to others, they demonstrate their social ability and how they relate to others. Dialogue brings the story to life.

You can develop character and plot through dialogue, as well as deepen any other aspect of your story. It is a critical part of fiction writing and can be hard to master, even if you are experienced in writing other things.

But don't worry. You can learn the basics of dialogue and then decide how far you want to take your expertise.

Some writers use it extensively, and others sparingly. Some authors start their writing process with dialogue, saying they 'hear' their characters talking and 'take dictation,' before expanding the story further.

From a reader perspective, some love a lot of dialogue while others prefer narrative and exposition. Some want deep authenticity in character voice, with accents and vocal tics, and others prefer a light touch.

You can usually tell a writer's preference by the amount of white space on a page, as the punctuation of dialogue means many more lines on a page, compared to a denser paragraph of description or inner thought.

Dialogue reflects the author's voice, just as much as the characters'. You will discover your preference as a reader and as a writer through your author journey.

Dialogue is not just a transcript of people talking

While listening to people talking is a great way to research different voices, dialogue in a novel is not a natural conversation.

People don't communicate in perfect sentences. If you transcribe any conversation directly, it will be full of repetitions, filler words, hesitation or thinking words like 'um,' and doesn't necessarily make sense.

Your job in writing dialogue is to make conversation natural, but still respect the reader's experience.

Vary dialogue tags with character action

Some writing craft books say that you should only ever use basic dialogue tags — for example, 'Morgan said' or 'Jake said' — because the reader skips over them in the text, so they barely register as repetition.

But that advice is dated in the world of increased audio consumption.

It is obvious to the listener when a writer uses repetitive words in an audiobook, and hearing dialogue tags like 'said' over and over again can cause them to stop listening.

However, you don't have to replace 'said' with words like 'interjected' or 'spat' or 'whispered,' although those can be good options if the story demands it.

Instead, replace dialogue tags with character action, so the reader knows who is speaking. For example:

> Morgan walked over to the window and looked out at the sparkling blue waters. "The key is out there somewhere. We just have to find it."

Make it clear who is speaking… but don't overuse character names

"Hi Bob, how's the rocket this morning?" Jane said.

"Oh, hi Jane, it's looking good," Bob replied. "Just need to sort out the paint job."

"Have fun with that, Bob," Jane said, as she turned away and stepped into the portal.

It's clear to the reader who's speaking here, but it's like being bashed over the head with the repeated names and it feels clumsy. New writers will often use names inside dialogue and use them in tags as well, but it's not necessary.

Here's a new version.

Jane leaned over the bench. "Hi Bob, how's the rocket this morning?"

"Lookin' good." Bob grinned and pointed at the can of red paint by his feet. "Just need to sort out the paint job."

"Have fun with that." Jane turned away and stepped into the portal.

This uses action within dialogue. It's clear who is speaking and we're not overusing character names.

Use dialogue to move the plot forward

All sorts of interesting things can come up between characters through dialogue. For example, characters may be forced to resolve a conflict or work together to escape a situation or solve a puzzle.

Conflict in dialogue can bring the story alive, and relationship clashes portrayed through dialogue can be brutal. We often know how to hurt those we love with words.

One of my favorite TV series is *Succession*, about an ageing billionaire media mogul and the fight amongst his children as to who will succeed him as CEO. The dialogue between the four siblings as well as with the father, mother, and other family members, as well as between lovers and spouses, is savage, but as such, resonates as true.

Subtext

Subtext is the true meaning under surface spoken words and is revealed through character action. How often do you say, "I'm fine," when you're actually angry and show that anger in different ways, like slamming a door?

Reading screenplays can help with learning how to write good dialogue because they only show action and dialogue between characters in a setting, rather than explaining inner thoughts. Seeing the pairing of a dialogue line with an action will give you ideas for how you can create the same kind of subtext on a page.

Dictate or read dialogue out loud

If you dictate your story, you might find your dialogue is more natural from the start. But if you write it, you are likely to find during editing that your dialogue is overly formal.

Read it aloud, and you'll spot the issues. I always have to rewrite dialogue in my edit!

Beware of 'on the nose' dialogue

'On the nose' dialogue is a screenwriting term and refers to telling instead of showing. It's when characters say what they feel and what has happened, instead of showing it through action.

A (very) on the nose example might be:

"I'm so sad," Marie said.

"Is it because your husband just left you for another woman?" Janice replied.

Compare that to:

> Marie sat on the edge of the sofa shaking with sobs, her hands covering her face as if to shut out the world.
>
> Janice rubbed her friend's back slowly, in a soothing motion, like she did with her children. "He's a bastard," she said, an edge of steel in her voice. "Let her have him. You deserve better."

Dialect and speech mannerisms

While it is a good idea to differentiate your main characters, at least, through their speech patterns, dialect, character voice, and mannerisms, it's up to you how far you want to go with this.

Some writers have made a career out of writing effectively with dialect — for example, *Trainspotting* by Irvine Welsh in Scots English. Some consider it important for representation and the world of the book to immerse the reader in a different language.

Other writers consider dialect and speech mannerisms as seasoning, rather than differentiating every sentence of every fragment of dialogue. In *IT*, by Stephen King, one of the main characters has a stutter, but King portrays it with a light touch. The reader can skim over the words without stopping too much on the repeated stuttering dialogue.

You can also use verbal description, which will help with adaptation to audio. One author I know was appalled to find her novel with an Irish protagonist narrated with an accent like a leprechaun, instead of the gentle lilt she had imagined. The assumption of 'Irish' without further descriptors had been taken too far into cliché during adaptation.

Don't use fake dialogue to introduce back story

We've all heard or read this type of dialogue.

> "Hey Mary, isn't your sister coming over tonight? You know, the one who married that criminal from down south who is getting out of jail soon and promised to kill her when he got out?"

Clearly, Mary would know about her sister's past, so this dialogue is a clumsy way of providing back story about a character who will arrive soon, and telegraphs plot in an inept fashion.

Find another way to weave in back story. It might take more words, but it will be a better book.

It's dialogue, not monologue

If you have paragraphs of one character speaking, then it's probably an info dump, or you haven't considered what action could occur at the same time.

What are the other characters doing while this character is speaking? What could be happening while they talk? Are there other ways you could communicate the necessary information to the reader without using this much dialogue?

Swearing and curse words

You need to make a decision about swearing and profanity early in your author career, because readers are particular about what curse words they allow. You can ritually murder children or blow up a hospital in your fiction and get away with it, but if you use a surprise f-bomb when you don't usually include cursing, you'll get angry comments and one-star reviews.

I know because this happened to me, so I decided not to use cursing in my books at all.

Some authors will say, 'Well, my characters are New York cops [or insert character type here] so they have to swear.' But you can write authentic characters without swearing and readers won't even notice.

Of course, you can absolutely curse all you like in your fiction. Use any language you choose — just be consistent. If your characters swear, make it clear from your first book, and readers will self-select for the level they want to read.

Questions:

- In what way do you want to use dialect and speech mannerisms in your story? Why are you making this choice?
- Will you use curse words in your dialogue?
- Select a dialogue-heavy scene from your manuscript and check it against the potential problems listed in this chapter. Which do you need to watch out for, and how can you fix them?
- Similarly, are there tools like subtext or action tags that you could be using more effectively? Are you using dialogue to move the plot forward and/or reveal character?

Resources:

- *Dialogue: The Art of Verbal Action for Page, Stage, and Screen* — Robert McKee

- *How to Write Dazzling Dialogue: The Fastest Way to Improve Any Manuscript* — James Scott Bell

- Dialogue Doctor Jeff Elkins, podcast and resources — www.DialogueDoctor.com

- Writing dialogue and character voice with Jeff Elkins. Interview with transcript — www.TheCreativePenn.com/elkins

3.6 Plot: What happens in the story?

> "Every story is about a character who gets into trouble and then tries to get out of it."
>
> —*Kurt Vonnegut*

Plot is what happens to the characters in your story. It's the events of your book.

A plot point can be small, like receiving a letter and showing the emotional impact of its contents. Or it can be significant, like a bomb going off in central London. Your plot points will be determined by the type of story and your creative vision.

Some writers start with story ideas about plot and work backward to character, theme, and everything else. Others come to plot later. It doesn't matter. However you do it, your book needs plot!

How do you come up with plot ideas?

Every writer has their strengths and some are brimming with ideas about plot. But what if you're struggling for what happens in your story?

Consider the following places to start.

If you have a character already, what do they want? How can you stop your character from getting what they want? What obstacles can you put in their way? How can you make things more difficult? How will they overcome those obstacles or challenges in order to achieve their goal?

How does one thing lead to another?

In *The Hunger Games*, the inciting incident is when Prim, Katniss's sister, is chosen for The Reaping. Katniss volunteers to take her place. This one decision (plot point) leads to the events of the games (a load of other plot points).

Each action by a character (or plot point) can lead to unexpected consequences. In *A Game of Thrones*, Cersei Lannister goes up against the High Sparrow, a religious leader who humbles her in front of her people as punishment. As she walks through the streets naked, pelted with rubbish by the people of King's Landing, we know this moment (plot point) will lead to some kind of violent retribution (plot point).

Cersei's revenge when it comes (plot point) is a double-edged sword. Every action — every plot point — leads to something else. Every choice has a consequence.

Setting can also inspire plot. If you have a setting in mind, what kind of interesting things could happen there?

I was inspired to write my crime thriller *Desecration* when I visited the Hunterian Museum in London. The atrium has glass cabinets full of macabre anatomical specimens in jars, and I imagined a recently dead body lying in the middle of it all. The story idea started with the setting, which then inspired aspects of plot, which then gave rise to characters.

If you're interested in a topic, research it through books and documentaries and note down events that could turn into plot. *A Game of Thrones* draws inspiration from the bloody history of medieval England. Fifteenth-century prince Edward of Lancaster inspired the character of King Joffrey Baratheon, and various battles in the novels were based on the Wars of the Roses.

The relics of the Apostles inspired my thriller *Stone of Fire*, and some of the bones lie in cathedrals around Europe and the Middle East. Morgan and Jake have to retrieve powerful stones carried by the Apostles in a race against time, so the plot was driven by the places they visited on the adventure. My research drove both setting and plot.

Consider your favorite books, films, and TV shows. Many of them might use similar plot points, but the originality is in the characters, the world, and what the writer brings that is unique.

Plot is also determined by the reader's expectation for your genre. If you're writing a mystery, there will be a murder and the plot points will relate to finding the murderer. If you're writing a romance, you need specific plot points around how the characters meet, what obstacles they face, and how they overcome them to reach a happy ending.

Go fill the creative well. Read, watch movies, check the news, or social media. Notice what is happening in the world — then turn those things into plot ideas.

The main plot and the subplots, or A and B plots

There is usually one overarching main plot that drives a story.

In *A Game of Thrones*, it is the fight for the throne of Westeros. In *The Hunger Games*, Katniss must win the games in order to survive. In *Map of Shadows*, Sienna and the Mapwalker team must find the map before the Shadow Cartographers use it to open a portal and reclaim Earthside.

The subplots are everything else that goes on, and there are usually lots of subplots involving different characters.

In *A Game of Thrones*, one subplot is Tyrion's relationship with his brother, Jamie, and with the rest of the Lannisters. This relationship enriches the characters, introduces new plot threads, and intensifies the overall emotional resonance of the novel. We all understand family conflict! Tyrion also has a comedic subplot with the mercenary Bronn who starts out as a sword for hire but ends up as a loyal friend.

In *The Hunger Games*, Katniss's relationship with Peeta is a romance subplot. In *Map of Shadows*, there is a romantic subplot between Sienna and the rebel Borderlander Finn, as well as a subplot involving Sienna's mastery of her Mapwalking magic — and the price she must pay to use it.

You can use subplots to develop character and introduce other elements that engage the reader in the world of the story. Many authors end up developing side characters and subplots into stories of their own.

Raise the stakes

> "Story is about how the things that happen in the plot affect the protagonist and how he or she changes internally as a result."
>
> —*Lisa Cron, Story Genius*

There has to be a reason that characters are driven into a plot. They have to be motivated enough to go through with whatever you throw at them. The stakes have to be high enough.

What might they lose?

What might they gain?

In the opening chapters of my thriller *Stone of Fire*, a shadowy group of assassins attack Morgan Sierra at her office in Oxford, seeking the powerful stone her archaeologist father gave her before he was killed.

Morgan fights back, but her only goal is to get out alive. She has no interest in joining the wider mission of the ARKANE secret agency investigating the supernatural mystery of the stones.

But then her twin sister and little niece are abducted and Morgan must find the stones before the clock ticks down to their fiery end. The stakes are suddenly much higher and Morgan will do anything for her family.

I write thrillers, so the stakes are often life and death, but stakes can be emotional or social or psychological as well. One reason YA novels are so powerful is because when we're young adults everything feels so intense and life-changing. I still have my journals from age fifteen, and the stakes were clearly high, even though I look back and think differently now.

Will the boy I fancy ask me out? Will I get good grades in my exams — and if I don't, is my life over?

Does God have a plan for me — and if I have sex before marriage, am I going to hell? (I was in an evangelical Christian youth group at the time, so much of my journal is about God — and boys!)

The stakes in your novel will depend on the genre you write, your characters, and your creative direction.

Try/fail cycles

A story won't be satisfying to the reader if your character wants something, tries to get it, and achieves their goal straight away.

The character needs to go through multiple try/fail cycles.

They need to attempt to get to their goal, fail because something or someone stops them, then try again, and so on, until they finally achieve their goal, or fail completely — depending on the kind of story it is.

The TV medical drama *House* has these try/fail cycles in every episode. A patient is admitted to the hospital with a horrific disease. As the clock ticks toward their gruesome end, Dr House and his team must discover what's wrong before it's too late. There are try/fail cycles each time in the diagnostic process until the final attempt when the patient is treated successfully.

In your story, make sure the protagonist doesn't get what they want the first — or even the second — time.

Plot twists and other ways of surprising the reader

Plot twists are elements of a story that surprise the reader. The twist might delight them or it might horrify them, but whatever it is, the story goes in a direction that they did not expect.

James Patterson goes into detail on this in his MasterClass video course. As he outlines, he considers multiple endings to each scene, and says, "When there are big plot points, discard your first idea, and your second, and your third. Otherwise, it will be obvious to the reader."

The end of the first book (and TV series) of *A Game of Thrones* has a twist in the form of a main character dying unexpectedly. No spoilers! We are led to believe a particular character is the protagonist and the most likely victor for the throne. When the brutal twist comes, it scatters the other characters to the wind and sends the story in a new direction. This happens so many times in the TV adaptation of *A Game of Thrones*. It really is a masterclass in twists and misdirection.

Gone Girl by Gillian Flynn starts out as a murder mystery, but the use of an unreliable narrator turns it into a psychological thriller. While this technique was surprising when the book came out, the number of subsequent 'lookalike' books has made it much harder to surprise readers with an unreliable narrator.

But it's okay — not all stories need twists and surprises, and you don't have to supply them to satisfy readers. So if it's not your thing, don't worry!

Obligatory scenes

Expectations about a book shape how your reader experiences the story.

If they bought a sweet romance with a happy couple on the cover, then they expect something different to an epic fantasy, a horror novel, or literary fiction.

There are conventions in every genre; in *The Story Grid*, Shawn Coyne describes these as 'obligatory scenes.' The reader expects them and will be disappointed if they are missing from the book.

As a thriller reader, I expect a scene where the hero is at the mercy of the villain. A classic mystery reader will expect a scene where the dead body is discovered, and one near the end where the detective unmasks the murderer.

Romance readers expect a scene where the lovers meet, then various events stop them getting together, and at some point, a first kiss, or something more explicit if it's erotica.

In horror novels, genre fans know that when the protagonist thinks evil is vanquished and everything is going to be okay, evil will probably return one more time.

Consider what you expect as a reader in the books you love the most. How can you incorporate such obligatory scenes with an original spin?

Tropes

Tropes are part of what readers enjoy in a genre. They are an aspect of the story that makes a reader feel like this is the book for them. They are more granular than the obligatory scene, and can have aspects of character, plot, setting, or theme.

A character trope might be The Chosen One in fantasy — for example, Harry Potter, Neo in *The Matrix*, or Luke Skywalker in *Star Wars*.

A setting trope might be a ruined castle on a moonlight night for Gothic horror.

A plot trope might be 'enemies to lovers' for a romance.

But tropes will not make your writing cliché. As ever, it is the personal spin we bring to a story that makes it original.

We all have different aspects of story that we love, things that are catnip to our reader's mind and creative soul. Dr Jennifer Lynn Barnes has a wonderful talk she gives on the topic of the "Id List," teaching writers how to identify the elements of story that make it irresistible to you and your readers. The Id is the most primitive and instinctual part of us, the aspect that shouts, 'Yes, I love this!'

We all have different things on our Id Lists. Some of mine include tombs and crypts, relationships between sisters, violent thunderstorms, ancient manuscripts in hidden libraries, religious relics, maps and cartography, priests and nuns, fathers and daughters, ancient Egypt, scars, apocalyptic evil, and much more!

Create your own Id List and include aspects of them in your novel.

Flashbacks

Readers experience your story in a linear fashion, from beginning to end. If you halt the forward momentum with a flashback, you interrupt that flow. You drag the reader out of the moment of the story.

There are sometimes good reasons to use flashbacks, but many new writers overuse them to illustrate back story, when it isn't necessary.

If you want to write a scene from the past, consider whether you really need it, or whether there is another way to portray that aspect of the character's back story — for example, provide hints in different places, or memories that emerge during the plot, rather than all at once.

Open questions and open loops

> "Don't give the audience four.
> Give them two plus two."

—*Andrew Stanton, filmmaker, WALL-E, Toy Story*

Readers are smart, especially voracious readers in a particular genre. You don't need to hit them over the head with the obvious. You don't need a huge signpost spelling out meaning.

In fact, you want to do the opposite.

Open loops leave the reader desperate to close them.

Provoke questions in the reader's mind and they will read on to find the answer.

When you close one loop, open another.

If you answer a question, make sure there are others still waiting to be dealt with.

This desire to close the circle and answer all the questions will drive the reader through the novel, and by the end, they can feel satisfied that everything has been tied up with a neat bow. Unless, of course, you're writing a series and want to pull them into the next book with more open loops.

Read one of the books you love and note the open questions and open loops that pull you through the story. Where are they placed? How many open loops does the writer have at one time? How can you use the same technique with your plot?

Foreshadowing

Foreshadowing is including something earlier in the story that makes sense later on. When the reader gets to that later point, they have a satisfying 'aha' moment.

But don't worry, it's not complicated to do this.

The reader experiences your story in a linear fashion, but you don't need to write it that way. Once you've finished, go back in during the editing process and add foreshadowing to deepen the reader experience.

In *Destroyer of Worlds*, Asha Kapoor wants to use a mythological weapon at the Kumbh Mela, the largest Hindu pilgrimage in the world. The weapon is hidden on a statue of Shiva Nataraja, where the Hindu god dances the universe into destruction surrounded by a circle of flames.

In Asha's first scene, she trails her fingers through candle flames at the bedside of her dying father, and I use the metaphor of flame throughout, foreshadowing her ultimate fiery end.

You can also set up your character for later aspects of plot. In *The Hunger Games*, Katniss uses a bow and arrow to keep herself alive. In the opening chapters, we see her hunting for food, demonstrating her expertise with the weapon, so it's not a surprise when she later uses it to kill.

Losing the plot

If you're an outliner, you might never experience this. But as a discovery writer, I tend to 'lose the plot' at some point in every first draft.

I usually have enough in my head to write to around 20,000 words and then I grind to a halt. The story is a chaotic mess and I need to figure out what the hell is happening.

I print out what I have so far — often a load of random scenes — and read it through, noting down anything that might be a jumping off point to something else. There will also be open questions about characters and conflict, or I consider how a setting could be used more effectively for the story, or anything else that comes to mind.

You can also put the story away for a week to get some distance and then read through what you have again. Or do some more research about the ideas, places, and people that fuel the story. Trust the creative process and something will emerge. You will find the plot again!

Questions:

- If you aren't already brimming with plot ideas, how might you come up with them?
- What is your main plot?
- What are your subplots?
- How can you raise the stakes so the plot is more engaging to the reader?
- How can you incorporate try/fail cycles into your plot?
- Do the books you enjoy incorporate twists and surprises? How could you work a plot twist into your novel?
- Consider what you expect as a reader in the books you love the most. How can you incorporate such obligatory scenes with an original spin?
- What are some tropes that you love in books, film, and TV? How can you incorporate tropes to satisfy readers while still making them fresh?
- What are some of the story elements that are catnip to you as a reader and as an author? What aspects go on your Id List?

- Do your favorite books use flashbacks? When might they be effective in your novel? Are there other ways of presenting the same story elements?

- Read one of the books you love and note the open questions and open loops that pull you through the story. How can you do the same with your plot?

- Which elements of your plot or characters could you foreshadow early in your story?

- What questions can you ask yourself or your novel if you lose the plot?

Resources:

- *Mastering Plot Twists: How to Use Suspense, Targeted Storytelling Strategies, and Structure to Captivate Your Readers* — Jane K. Cleland

- *Plot and Structure: Techniques and Exercises for Crafting a Plot that Grips Readers from Start to Finish* — James Scott Bell

- *Story Genius: How to Use Brain Science to Go Beyond Outlining and Write a Riveting Novel* — Lisa Cron

- *The Story Grid: What Good Editors Know* — Shawn Coyne
- List of TV tropes — www.tvtropes.org
- MasterClass video course with James Patterson — www.TheCreativePenn.com/masterclass
- "The Clues to a Great Story," Andrew Stanton TED talk — www.ted.com/talks/andrew_stanton_the_clues_to_a_great_story
- "Writing for Your Id," Dr Jennifer Lynn Barnes talk for Romance Writers America (RWA) — www.TheCreativePenn.com/idlist
- "The Shapes of Stories" video with Kurt Vonnegut — www.youtube.com/watch?v=oP3c1h8v2ZQ

3.7 Conflict

"Conflict is the reason your character can't have what he wants. If your character could have what he wants, then you have no book!"

—*Debra Dixon, GMC: Goal, Motivation, Conflict*

Conflict is all the things that your characters must face in order to reach their goal. It's everything that gets in the way of them achieving what they want.

Conflict also keeps readers engaged with your story because humans can't help but watch conflict play out. Witnessing conflict helps us figure out how we should act in the world in order to stay safe. It's a psychological and physical necessity.

There are different kinds of conflict, and you can layer them all into your story.

External conflict

These are situations where characters face challenges from the external world. If the challenge is big enough, it can drive the plot of the entire story.

In *Risen Gods*, a tsunami is about to destroy the city

where Ben and Lucy live in New Zealand. This kind of natural phenomenon also drives 'human versus nature' disaster movies like *Armageddon*, and 'human versus creature' stories like *Jaws* or *Jurassic Park*.

Conflict can also be supernatural. In *A Game of Thrones*, the entire race of humans is threatened by the rising of the White Walkers and the army of the dead, as well as the advance of winter. In *The Hunger Games*, Katniss must tackle the challenges and conflict of the game to survive. *Ex Machina* features humans versus technology, and there are countless stories of humans versus aliens.

External conflict can also be about society. For example, *Brave New World* by Aldous Huxley is set in a futuristic state where citizens have a wonderful life in many ways, but are kept docile by the drug Soma, and there are strict rules around how to live. Conflict comes when characters question and rebel against the constricts of society.

In *A Game of Thrones*, Queen Cersei finds herself in conflict with the High Sparrow, who leads a militant religious sect that takes control of King's Landing. Cersei finds herself in conflict with a belief system and must submit to it, before finding her answer.

Interpersonal conflict

This is conflict between people. It might be within a family, or between friends or partners, or between different groups.

In *A Game of Thrones,* the Lannister family is brimming with conflict between the siblings — Cersei, Jamie, and Tyrion — with love, hate, and violence between them all at different times.

The TV series *Succession* portrays family conflict through the actions of each sibling as they fight to succeed their father in business — and win his love.

The Walking Dead TV series layers interpersonal over external conflict. The survivors of the zombie apocalypse fight each other as much as the walking dead.

Internal conflict

This is conflict within the character based on their situation and how they respond to it. The conflict stems from the influence of culture and family, their experiences and values, as well as their personality, and how they choose to act based on the plot situation.

In *A Game of Thrones,* Arya Stark trains to be an assassin, but in order to become a true 'faceless man,' she has to give up her family name. Is she a Stark or is she no one?

In *Risen Gods*, Ben Henare is Maori, but he doesn't believe in the mythology of his people. He has to overcome his doubts about faith in order to ultimately triumph.

Use all types of conflict in your story

If your story is not engaging, try adding some conflict. Consider, especially, whether your novel has both internal and external conflict.

If your original premise focuses heavily on plot, you might want to explore internal and interpersonal conflicts to enhance the emotional drama of your story. If your story is more focused on personal development, it might benefit from a shot of external conflict along the way.

Questions:

- Can you identify the different types of conflict in the books you love or the books that are like what you're writing?

- What would make the situation worse for your characters in each of the categories? How could you layer or amplify the conflict further?

Resources:

- *The Conflict Thesaurus: A Writer's Guide to Obstacles, Adversaries, and Inner Struggles* — Angela Ackerman and Becca Puglisi

- *GMC: Goal, Motivation, Conflict: The Building Blocks of Good Fiction* — Debra Dixon

3.8 Openings and endings

Your opening will determine whether the reader buys your book.

Your ending will determine whether they buy the next one, write a good review, tell their friends, and spread the word.

Openings

The goal of your opening is to keep the reader turning the pages. They need to feel like this is the story for them.

It must engage them immediately, but also give a clear indication of the genre, so the reader knows they want to commit their time and money to the experience. You also want to open questions in the reader's mind so they want to read on.

My thriller *One Day in New York* opens as follows:

> For all the hypervigilance of New Yorkers at the slightest possibility of terrorism, they embrace anything that could be construed as modern art. That's why no one reported the man constructing a strong wooden cross on The High Line that afternoon, next to a section

that overlooked the Hudson River to the west.

Later in the scene, an old woman is crucified on that cross by the Confessors, who seek the powerful relic of an angel. By the end of the scene, the reader is left wondering who the woman is, who the Confessors are, and why they want this relic so much. They also know this is a thriller with religious — and perhaps supernatural — elements. They know the setting is New York, and all those things make a particular type of reader want to continue the story.

The opening is even more important in an era of ebook sampling. I'm a voracious reader and usually read three to five books per week. I read fiction in bed every night and it's how I spend a lot of my leisure time. A day spent reading is a day well spent!

I only read fiction in ebook format these days, and here's how I shop.

I find out about a book somehow — through social media, or a podcast, or a recommendation, or browsing in a physical bookstore. It might also be through browsing categories on Amazon, or through a recommendation email from a promotional site.

If I like the look of the cover and title, I read the description.

If it sounds like my kind of thing, I download a sample. If you're not an ebook reader, then a sample is a certain number of pages from the beginning of the book. The length of the sample is determined by the length of the book, so it might only be a few chapters.

If I already know that I like the author's books, I might buy immediately, but 95 percent of the time, I download a sample. I have several hundred samples on my Kindle at any one time. If the book is not available on Kindle, I might add it to my Wishlist and revisit in a few months' time to see if it's out in ebook yet.

When I want to read a novel, I go through my samples and start reading one of them. If I'm not engaged in the first few pages, I delete the sample. If I read to the end, I buy the book and continue reading.

The same is true of a paperback reader who picks up a physical book in a store. They might read the back and a few pages and then decide whether to buy.

The same is also true of an agent or a publisher if you're considering traditional publishing.

So the opening is important, but don't worry, you don't need to write the first chapter first. Come back to it later if you're struggling.

Endings

If the ending of a story strikes the wrong note, the reader is left unsatisfied, even if they loved the rest of the story.

The ending must complete the reader's experience and leave them with the sense that 'yes, this is how it should have ended.' Whatever the genre, you want your reader to give a sigh of happy satisfaction after a well-told story — especially if you want them to order your next book!

Genre readers have expectations of endings. If you promise a happy-ever-after, then you better provide one. If you're writing an epic fantasy quest, your band of travelers better find whatever they seek by the end, even if some of them are lost along the way.

I love supernatural horror novels. I expect a high body count and some seriously evil characters and plenty of bad things happening. But I want good to (ultimately) triumph and vanquish evil. I want someone to slay the monster, and I want a glimmer of hope at the end.

If you like books like this, *The Stand* by Stephen King, *Ararat* by Christopher Golden, and *The Deep* by Michaelbrent Collings are perfect examples of a satisfying ending, at least in my opinion as a horror reader.

Some of the most memorable endings are bittersweet. No spoilers, but consider *Me Before You* by JoJo Moyes, *The Notebook* by Nicholas Sparks, or the movie *Thelma and Louise*. They each end perfectly for the story they tell.

Disappointing endings are often those that feel like they don't 'fit'.

Surprise can be good, but only if it also feels inevitable. While Stephen King is one of my favorite authors, I find the ending of *Under the Dome* problematic. It was a surprise — but for me, it didn't fit.

Your ending must also tie up loose ends, close open loops, and answer questions for the reader. If you're writing a series, then, of course, you can continue some story questions into the next book, but for the reader to feel satisfied, you need some level of closure at the end of each.

Questions:

- Examine the openings of the books you love. What makes them effective in keeping the reader turning the pages?

- What are some different openings for your book? Think of at least three options. Could the story open later in the plot? What would be the impact of opening in a different place?

- What endings do you remember as being 'just right'? What can you learn from those ending?

- What endings jarred you as a reader? Why did you feel that way?

- Do you already know how your story will end? How can you make that ending as effective as possible?

Resources:

- *Your First Page: First Pages and What They Tell Us about the Pages that Follow Them*
  — Peter Selgin

- *The First Five Pages: A Writer's Guide to Staying Out of the Rejection Pile*
  — Noah Lukeman

- *The Last Fifty Pages: The Art and Craft of Unforgettable Endings* — James Scott Bell

3.9 Setting and world-building: Where does the story happen?

All story happens somewhere. Your job as a writer is to evoke that setting in the mind of the reader.

It might be a space station in another galaxy, a claustrophobic apartment in an over- crowded street, or an underground city held together with magic. There are endless possibilities, which is why setting and world-building can be so much fun!

What is a setting? What is a world?

A scene happens in a setting.

The Hobbit by J.R.R. Tolkien opens as follows:

> In a hole in the ground there lived a hobbit. Not a nasty, dirty, wet hole filled with the ends of worms and an oozy smell, nor yet a dry, bare, sandy hole with nothing in it to sit down on or to eat: it was a hobbit-hole, and that means comfort.

The setting is the hobbit-hole, and the reader is soon introduced to Bilbo Baggins, Gandalf the wizard, and a host of dwarves heading off on an adventure.

This setting is only one place within Tolkien's sprawling world of Middle-earth, and his stories follow characters from the different races who live there. The reader experiences aspects of the entire world, but each character may only see a part of it.

If your story is set in the current world in modern times, you won't have to go into as much detail as Tolkien. But you still need to evoke a sense of place in the reader's mind, whatever kind of story you write.

World-building — how far should you go?

Some writers love world-building and will spend more time on that than anything else. Others will use a sense of place to underpin plot, character, and theme, but feel no need to create detailed maps and descriptions that don't appear in the novel.

Once again, only you can decide what you need for your story and how much time to spend on it.

However deep you decide to go, consider the following aspects of world-building and how they might influence character and plot.

Time period: When is the story set? Or does the action take place across multiple times?

Geography: What are the physical features of the world? What are the most significant places? What's the weather like?

Flora and fauna: What kinds of animals and plants are in the world? Are there any fantastical or magical creatures?

People and culture: What kinds of people populate the world? What cultural elements impact the characters the most? Consider religion, hierarchy and class tensions, gender differences, politics and government, education, business, language, law, and food. How has the history of the world affected what it's like today?

Technology: What tools and technology are available? Consider weapons, communication, and how technology might affect the culture.

Magic systems: Is there a magic system and how does it work?

You can create whatever world you like, but it must make sense within the story you're telling. If you set rules and expectations with your world or your magic system, you must keep to them. If a synthetic human with an AI-powered brain suddenly appeared in Middle-earth, it wouldn't make any sense to the reader.

World-building can be a lot of fun, but beware spending so much time on it that you never write your novel. There is no point having hundreds of pages of notes about a fictional world when you never tell a story in it.

Discover the world as you write

You don't need to spend loads of time creating and planning and drawing maps and world-building up front if that is not your thing.

As a discovery writer, I find aspects of my world as I write, and figure out how to make them consistent as I progress through the first draft, or even much later in the edit.

When I started writing *Map of Shadows*, my story idea was that some people could walk through maps into a world that we had written out of our own. As I wrote, I researched extinct creatures and put them into the Borderlands, and then further out into the Uncharted. I found places we had destroyed or written out of history, as well as groups of people who had stumbled over the Border as refugees, and based elements of my story world around them. I researched ancient places and spun them into new settings as I needed them.

My characters needed magic, and I am a dark little soul, so I made the most powerful Mapwalkers use blood magic. I'm fascinated by tattoos — they appear in many of my books — so the Blood Mapwalkers tattooed maps of our world onto their skin to protect the portals from the Shadow Cartographers.

I love walking along the canal in Bath, so I wrote a scene for one of my characters there, and discovered through writing it that she could mapwalk through water courses — oceans, rivers, canals — and use rain as a weapon.

There is so much more in my Mapwalker world, but I did not invent it until I sat down to write. I had the bare bones of an opening scene and created the world as I wrote. As ever, you can choose the method that works for you.

Use specific and sensory detail

Consider this sentence: "Max and Puja sat in a bar." It has characters in a setting, but your mental image of what the people and the bar look like will be different to mine, or anyone else's. Our imagination is shaped by our nationality, race, culture, and religion, our age and lifestyle preferences, and how the names of the characters resonate.

Your job as an author is to manipulate the mind of the reader.

You need to describe the characters and the settings so the image in the reader's mind is what you want it to be.

Is the bar a dark cavern underground with sticky floors and peeling band flyers on the walls and the stink of tobacco embedded in collapsing furniture?

Is it on an open rooftop overlooking the ocean, with high metal tables and wild palm decoration, with the scent of frangipani flowers on the soft breeze?

I've been in both of those kinds of bars and they were very different situations!

When you write setting, consider all the physical senses: sight, sound, smell, touch, and taste. You can also include feelings, metaphors, or other aspects that bring depth to the setting.

You don't have to include each of these elements every time, but consider what might be important for that particular setting within your story.

I am a primarily visual writer and my first instinct is to write settings that a reader can 'see' in their mind. But I am an introvert and sensitive to sound, so I often wear noise-cancelling headphones. My settings are therefore less vivid in terms of sound and smell in particular, and I often add elements during the editing process to enrich the scenes in this way.

How much detail is too much detail?

Consider how you experience the world.

There are hundreds of thousands of things you could pay attention to every day — but you choose what's important and filter the world through that lens.

Do the same for your story.

Choose the details that matter to the characters, the plot, the theme, and anything else you want to underscore in each scene.

Readers instinctively understand that words on the page give weight to particular aspects depending on how important they are. As playwright Anton Chekhov said, "If you say in the first chapter that there is a rifle hanging on the wall, in the second or third chapter it absolutely must go off. If it's not going to be fired, it shouldn't be hanging there."

Of course, you can also use this to send the reader off in the wrong direction by over-emphasizing certain details as red herrings. A classic technique of the mystery writer!

Character emotion and setting

We all have emotional reactions to a setting. Since you are writing from a character's point of view, their emotional perspective will shape the description of the setting.

For example, the emergency room of a hospital would be experienced differently by a young mother of a child having an asthma attack than it would by an experienced middle-aged ER nurse who has worked there for years and seen it all before. Each character would notice different aspects of the hospital setting, and their emotional response would shape the description depending on whose POV you write from.

You can also use setting to underscore emotion. Many writers and filmmakers use rain and storms to emphasize aspects of emotion. A character stands at a graveside mourning in a rainstorm rather than on a sunny day surrounded by happy birdsong, unless the writer has a different emotional point to make.

Use setting to generate plot

A Game of Thrones by George R.R. Martin uses setting to influence plot and character in dramatic ways. The various family Houses come from different parts of the world and their cultures, landscapes, and even climates impact the characters and the plot.

The Wall separates the wild far north from the rest of the kingdom. It keeps the Wildlings and the White Walkers out — but what if it is breached? This story question is evoked by the setting and is played out across the series in a dramatic way, impacting the lives of major and minor characters alike.

My story ideas often come from setting and a sense of place. *Risen Gods* was inspired by the earthquake that struck the city of Christchurch, New Zealand in February 2011. The city was devastated, and friends of mine were caught up in the disaster. In the novel, Ben and Lucy are separated and as the Maori gods rise, they must travel the length of New Zealand to find each other and save the country from destruction.

As they make their separate ways north, their adventures and challenges are driven by setting. For example, Ben encounters a demon in an ice cave at Franz Josef Glacier, and Lucy witnesses the great ocean monster Te Wheke at the crossing of the Strait.

What if you want to include visuals of your world-building in your book?

Some authors like to include maps or diagrams that evoke the world in their novels. Tolkien's hand-drawn maps of Middle-earth are a great example and why many fantasy authors love to use maps.

You can use a site like Inkarnate.com to help create your own map, or work through a resource like *Fantasy Mapping: Drawing Worlds* by Wesley Jones.

You can also commission professionals to produce one. For *Risen Gods*, we commissioned a fantasy map of Aotearoa New Zealand with the geography of the country and the Maori mythological creatures and gods that Ben and Lucy face along the way.

> You can see the map at:
> www.TheCreativePenn.com/risengodsmap

You can use author-focused freelance hub Reedsy to find an illustrator, or sites like 99Designs, Fiverr, or Upwork.

What is a world bible?

A world bible contains all the supporting information about your world, from maps and culture details, to historical research, character lists and bios, key plot elements, and anything else you want to include. You can use it to keep track of characters and plot as well as refer to it as you write to check for consistency and mine it for future story ideas.

Some authors create hugely detailed world bibles that they populate to keep track of everything. Others keep a few pages of key aspects.

For my ARKANE thrillers, I copy and paste every finished book into one Vellum project (which I use for formatting) and use the Search function if I need to check something. You could also use Scrivener or any method of grouping the finished novels so you can search across them all.

Have you evoked setting in each scene?

Every writer has their strengths and weaknesses.

If you love character and dialogue, you might find that you have pages of writing in which amazing conversations happen, but there is no indication of where they take place, and no richness to the setting or the world.

You can save this step for the edit, but make sure the reader can tell where each scene happens as well as what happens to whom along the way, and the character's emotional reaction to the setting. Don't just have talking heads in an empty white room.

Questions:

- What do you know so far about the settings or world of your novel? What do you still need to find out?

- Are you excited about world-building *before* you write? Or is it something you want to discover in the writing process?

- Which of the various aspects of the world will be important for the plot, character development, and/or theme of your novel?

- Have you written specific and sensory detail about each setting to bring it to life? Or do you have talking heads in an empty white room?

- How have you used character emotion to underscore elements of your setting?

- Do you need (or want) to create a world bible? How might it help you?

- How will you balance world-building with writing the novel? How will you stop yourself from drowning in world-building if you find the process enjoyable?

Resources:

- *30 Days of Worldbuilding: An Author's Step-by-Step Guide to Building Fictional Worlds* — A. Trevena

- *Fantasy Mapping: Drawing Worlds* — Wesley Jones

- *Holly Lisle's Create a World Clinic* — Holly Lisle

- *Wonderbook: The Illustrated Guide to Creating Imaginative Fiction* — Jeff VanderMeer

- Interview on world-building with Angeline Trevena — www.TheCreativePenn.com/angeline

- Map creation site — www.inkarnate.com

- Find illustrators and other freelancers who specialize in working with authors — www.TheCreativePenn.com/reedsy

- Other freelance sites — Upwork.com, 99Designs.com, Fiverr.com

3.10 Author voice

"Your writing voice is the deepest possible reflection of who you are. The job of your voice is not to seduce or flatter or make well-shaped sentences. In your voice, your readers should be able to hear the contents of your mind, your heart, your soul."

—*Meg Rosoff*

In the early years of my author career, I would get really annoyed at workshops and courses that emphasized the importance of author voice without explaining what the hell it was and how I could find it.

But it is hard to grasp what it is when you're starting out.

Your author voice is what makes your writing *your* writing.

In many ways, it's indefinable, but over a number of books, over a number of years, you will discover it and your readers will learn to recognize it.

How to find examples of author voice

Pick two established authors in your preferred genre who have written at least ten novels each. Compare the first five chapters of their latest books and see if you can pick out aspects of their author voice and identify how they differ from each other.

Consider books you find memorable and think about what is distinctive about the author's voice. It might be a turn of phrase, or a theme that comes up repeatedly, or pacing, or the way they use dialogue. It can be so many things, which is why it's not something you can force, only discover in yourself over time as you write.

How can you find your author voice?

For me, it was about letting go of self-censorship and fear of judgment and allowing myself to write what I truly wanted to write without letting my inner critic shut me down.

The first book where I really found my voice was *Desecration*. It was my fifth novel, and that book means so much to me because I let myself be me. I needed time to discover my shadow side, and I only uncovered it through writing.

I had intended to write a straight police procedural, but my Muse doesn't roll that way. Part of my author voice is an aspect of the supernatural in pretty much everything I write as J.F. Penn. I just can't help myself!

Don't worry. You do not have to find your voice with your first novel.

In fact, you might not be able to.

But keep writing and you'll discover golden threads that link your body of work. That will be your author voice.

> "A polished rock is just the same as every other polished rock. Don't smooth all the edges out — they might be your voice."
>
> —Dean Wesley Smith,
> *The Stages of a Fiction Writer*

Questions:

- Pick two established authors in your preferred genre with a number of novels under their belts. Compare the first five chapters of their latest books. Can you pick out elements of their author voice?

- Do you have a sense of your author voice yet? Don't worry if you don't. It will emerge over time.

Resources:

- *Find Your Artistic Voice: The Essential Guide to Working Your Creative Magic*
  — Lisa Congdon

- *The Stages of a Fiction Writer: Know Where You Stand on the Path to Writing*
  — Dean Wesley Smith

- *Voice: The Secret Power of Great Writing*
  — James Scott Bell

- "How to write fiction: Meg Rosoff on finding your voice," *The Guardian*, 18 Oct 2011 — www.theguardian.com/books/2011/oct/18/how-to-write-fiction-meg-rosoff

3.11 Theme

Theme is what the story is *really* about. Not the surface events of the plot, but the underlying concepts or principles that you want to underscore as part of the novel.

My crime thriller *Desecration* opens with a murder in an anatomy museum and, on the surface, it's a detective story about the hunt for the killer. But that's just the plot. The theme is how the physical body defines us in life — and in death.

Some authors start with theme.

Some authors discover theme after they've written the first draft or later during the editorial process.

Still others may never understand their theme consciously, but find readers comment about things in reviews that reveal an underlying theme after all.

Start with the theme in mind

Some authors are clear on the theme from the beginning. For example, the impact of racism is clearly an important theme that resonates with many writers.

You can then construct characters and plot to fit the theme, making sure they echo the important points along the way.

But remember, readers are smart and they don't want to read a lecture in novel form. Beware of overstating theme through character monologues, or info dumps. Find ways to evoke theme so it emerges from the story naturally.

Discover your theme along the way

Desecration was inspired by visiting the Hunterian Museum at the Royal College of Surgeons in London. I had a visceral reaction, a churning in my gut, to the body parts in jars and the brutal instruments used to harvest them as I wondered about the people whose organs lay there.

But my reaction puzzled me.

I'm an organ donor and I don't believe my physical body holds anything of me once I'm dead. I'd love my body parts to be useful after my death, either through helping others to live, or for scientists and doctors to learn from. I don't think physical disability, deformity, or illness should define everything about a person.

So I wrote an opening scene where a young woman is found murdered in the center of the atrium, surrounded by body parts in jars. The story — and the theme — developed from there.

Your themes become part of your author voice

Your obsessions have power, and you will likely return to them again and again in your stories.

One of my recurring themes is good versus evil on the supernatural level. It underscores so many of my stories, and it's the theme of my favorite and most memorable books as a reader. *The Stand* by Stephen King is an epic tale of good versus evil, and I love John Connolly's Charlie Parker series for the same reason.

As a teenager, I was obsessed with stories of spiritual warfare, angels and demons, and the forces of light battling the realms of darkness. Although I have a master's degree in theology, I am not religious, but these things still shape my fiction. Even when I try to write something that is not supernatural, with no religious elements, I just can't help myself. My Muse loves what she loves, and I cannot deny her.

As readers, we return to authors we love because

their themes resonate with us at a deeper level, so lean into the themes that come up for you because it's likely that your readers love that about your writing.

> "The moment that you feel that, just possibly you're walking down the street naked, exposing too much of your heart and your mind and what exists on the inside, showing too much of yourself, that's the moment you may be starting to get it right."
>
> —Neil Gaiman, *Make Good Art*

You're writing a story, not a lecture

You don't need to be explicit about your theme. You don't need to state it anywhere or insert obvious monologue into the voice of a character. Readers are smart and they understand how story works.

Desecration is not a lecture on how the physical body defines us in life or in death. It's a murder mystery with engaging characters and a fast-moving plot, but along the way, I hope readers end up considering those deeper questions.

> "The more you wish to describe a Universal, the more minutely and truthfully you must describe a Particular."
>
> —Brenda Ueland, *If You Want to Write*

Deepen your theme in the editorial process

Your first draft is often about getting the story down as best you can. When you return to it in the editorial process, consider how you could deepen your theme by adding specific details around setting, or use symbols and metaphor to underscore theme without being obvious.

For example, say your story is about a teacher fighting corruption in a small town. She wants to give her students a chance to escape to a better life, a chance she feels she has lost. You can show corruption through the character of the police chief when he takes money from a criminal gang to turn a blind eye to their deeds, but how else could you underscore theme?

Perhaps the teacher takes her class outside to sit in the shade of an old apple tree one hot day in the autumn. The heart of the wood is rotten and there are maggots crawling in the fallen fruit, so they can't stay in the shade of its branches. Perhaps the teacher loves gardening and tends to the tree after the school day is over, working to restore its health and carve out its rotten heart.

In *Desecration*, one of the clues is an ivory Anatomical Venus, a carving of a beautiful woman with her body opened up as if on an anatomist's table. Such sculptures were used as teaching aids, but are also valuable art pieces, and fetish objects. The Anatomical Venus underscores the theme of the meaning of the physical body, as the viewer is drawn in by its beauty, but also repelled by the gruesome display of the cadaver's organs.

You can also use repeating images to underscore theme. In *Destroyer of Worlds*, Morgan and Jake have to find the pieces of a statue of Shiva Nataraja, depicting the god surrounded by flames as he both destroys the world and renews it. In my scenes with the antagonist Asha Kapoor, I use flames multiple times in her character arc to reiterate the theme of destruction by fire.

Questions:

- Do you know the theme you want to write about already? Don't worry if you don't. You can figure it out later.
- Think about the books you love. What are their themes?
- How can you evoke theme in your novel without lecturing the reader?
- How can you deepen your theme?

Resources:

- *If You Want to Write* — Brenda Ueland
- *Make Good Art* — Neil Gaiman
- *On Writing: A Memoir of the Craft* — Stephen King
- *Writing Your Story's Theme: The Writer's Guide to Plotting Stories That Matter* — K.M. Weiland

3.12 Book or story title

"I think of the titles first."

—*R.L. Stine, author of the Goosebumps series, with over 400 million sold*

Some authors start with the title, others find the title later, and that may change from book to book. If you publish independently, the title is your choice, but if you choose a traditional publishing deal, the title might be out of your hands, depending on the situation.

What kind of titles make you pick up a book?

Think about your behavior as a reader. How much does the title play a part in your decision to sample or buy?

If it's an author and series that I know I like, I will buy the book regardless of the title. John Connolly's Charlie Parker series, Douglas Preston and Lincoln Child's Pendergast series, and pretty much anything by Jonathan Maberry are on that list.

If I don't know the author, the title is often what

catches my eye. The book cover is less relevant as I shop for fiction on my black and white Kindle Paperwhite or my phone. The cover is thumbnail size, but the title has more space on the virtual page. In a physical bookstore, I notice the cover first and then the title, but I never read fiction in print anymore, so I might note down the title and look at it online later.

We all have our preferences in reading and I almost always sample fiction that implies a religious thriller angle. My library includes *Song of Kali* by Dan Simmons, *Angelology* by Danielle Trussoni, *Dreams of Gods and Monsters* by Laini Taylor, and many more with words in their titles that resonate with my particular catnip as a reader.

Go through the books on your shelf or device, especially those by authors you don't buy from based on name recognition.

Are there common words? Or a theme or emotional resonance that comes up multiple times?

Write a list of those words and weigh them up against your story for possible book title ideas.

Choose words that resonate with your genre. This might sound obvious, but there's a reason that words like 'love' or 'heart' come up in so many romance titles, while 'blood' and 'death' appear in so many thrillers, crime novels, and mysteries.

Make sure you give a nod to genre in your title and, when placed in context with the book cover, the reader will be clear on what type of book this is.

Use quotes or other book titles to inspire your own

My short story trilogy title *A Thousand Fiendish Angels* is based on a quote from Dante's *Inferno,* Canto VIII.

"I saw more than a thousand fiendish angels perching above the gates, enraged and screaming: 'Who is this one who comes, and without death, dares walk into the kingdom of the dead?'"

The title also resonates with the theme and genre, implying an element of dark fantasy and horror.

Many books take their titles from Shakespeare. *Brave New World* by Aldous Huxley is from *The Tempest,* and *The Fault in Our Stars* by John Green is from *Julius Caesar.*

Be careful with this approach. While titles themselves cannot be copyrighted (in English), you can't use brands or character names or other potentially protected intellectual property. Be especially careful about song lyrics. If you're unclear on what you can use, check out *How To Use Memorable Lyrics Without Paying a Fortune or a Lawyer* by Helen Sedwick and Jessica M. Brown.

Find the title within your book

During the editing process, you might find a line of text that works well as a title. Keep a note of it and see if it resonates as a title later.

Use a character name or type

The Harry Potter series uses his name in every book title, and *The Girl on the Train* spawned a glut of thrillers with 'girl' in the title, proving this option can also be overdone.

If you're writing in a series, think about multiple book titles

Series books tend to have titles that link them together in some way. For example, my Mapwalker trilogy includes *Map of Shadows*, *Map of Plagues*, and *Map of the Impossible*, which have a repetition in the titles.

For my Brooke and Daniel crime thriller series, I wrote *Desecration* and then settled on words beginning with *D*, so the next books were *Delirium* and *Deviance*. I have a list of other interesting words beginning with *D* for possible sequels.

You can even imply the number of books. For example, Sue Grafton's alphabet crime series started with *A is for Alibi*.

Use a working title during the writing process

You don't have to decide on your final title right away. Sometimes it's best just to give your project a working title so you have something to call it, and then finalize it later on.

My first novel started out as *Mandala*, then became *Pentecost*, and later *Stone of Fire*. What started out as *Day of the Martyr* turned into *Tomb of Relics* after I'd finished the draft.

If all else fails, change the title later

My first three novels were originally called *Pentecost*, *Prophecy*, and *Exodus*. A few years after publication, I re-edited, re-titled, and re-released them as *Stone of Fire*, *Crypt of Bone*, and *Ark of Blood*, removing the confusion about whether they were Christian fiction (they're not) while still retaining the action-adventure thriller vibe.

Questions:

- Examine the books on your shelf or your device, especially those by authors you don't buy from based on name recognition. What are some of the common words used in titles? Is there a theme or resonance across them? Write down a list of those words and weigh them up against your story.

- Have a look at the top 100 books in your genre. Write down the titles and see if you can find commonalities.

- What are some other ways you can come up with book titles?

Resources:

- Interview with R.L. Stine on The Author Hour — www.theauthorhour.com/r-l-stine

- *How To Use Memorable Lyrics Without Paying a Fortune or a Lawyer* — Helen Sedwick and Jessica M. Brown

3.13 Language versus story and tools versus art

> "I don't think I'm a writer. I think I'm a storyteller… The words aren't always perfect."
>
> —*Stephenie Meyer, author of the Twilight saga, with over 160 million copies sold*

You can write a commercially successful novel without writing beautiful literary sentences.

You can win an award with beautiful literary sentences and only sell a few thousand copies.

While many writers say they want both outcomes, you are unlikely to achieve critical acclaim and commercial success with the same novel. Only you can decide what is most important, and you can, of course, change that goal with each book you write.

Tools versus art

You need to learn how to use the tools of the writing craft — how to structure a story, how to write sentences that communicate your meaning, how to use grammar and punctuation to achieve the effect you intend.

But the *art* of the writing craft is another aspect entirely.

There are some books you read for the sheer beauty of language rather than the story. There are novels you read and wonder how the author created such literary beauty with the same letters we all have at our disposal.

Learn the tools so you can write this story, then you can spend the rest of your life perfecting your art if you want to.

What is a 'good' book? What is 'quality'?

A 'good' book is whatever that means to the reader.

A 'quality' book is whatever that means to the reader.

Don't judge other authors for what they choose to write.

Don't judge readers for what they want to read.

Focus on what you want to achieve with your novel and learn the craft you need to satisfy your readers.

Questions:

- Would you rather sell millions of books to millions of happy readers who love your stories? Or would you rather win a literary prize and (most likely) sell fewer copies?

- What do you think is a 'good' book? What do you think is a 'quality' book? Examine your bookshelves for what you buy and read, rather than an intellectual response.

Resources:

- "Stephenie Meyer: A New J. K. Rowling?" *Time Magazine,* 24 April 2008 — content.time.com/time/subscriber/article/0,33009,1734838,00.html

Part 4: Writing the First Draft

4.1 Attitude to the first draft

> "Don't be so afraid of writing badly that you don't write at all."
>
> —SARK, *Succulent Wild Woman*

It's time.

You've spent long enough preparing — maybe even procrastinating. At some point, you have to start writing.

Perhaps you already have pages of story fragments.

Perhaps you have nothing but an idea in your head.

It doesn't matter what you have before you start. At some point, you must start writing the first draft and wrangle your chaos of thoughts and words into something that can be read by someone else.

You must take this step, or you will never finish your novel.

Remember the iceberg. You don't need to know everything before you start. Just get going and figure the rest out later.

Your first draft won't be perfect, and you certainly

don't need to show it to anyone, but at least you will have something to work with.

Of course, things will change in the editing process, but there's a tremendous feeling of satisfaction when the first draft is done.

That feeling is your goal.

Before we get into the practicalities of writing, here are two ideas that helped me when I started out.

Write the "shitty first draft"

> "For me and most of the other writers I know, writing is not rapturous. In fact, the only way I can get anything written at all is to write really, really shitty first drafts."
>
> —Anne Lamott, *Bird By Bird*

One of the life-changing moments in my writing life was when I learned that the first draft is just that — the *first* draft.

A reader will never see it. An editor should probably never see it.

This draft is for you. Once it's finished, you can start editing and make the manuscript better on the next pass.

The myth of writing is that an author sits down and creates a perfect, fully formed sentence on the page, followed by another and another, until they have finished a superb story in one attempt.

But that's not how writing works.

You will never see the first draft of your favorite book and, as a new writer, you can only compare someone else's finished novel to your first draft writing. That's not a fair comparison, so try not to do it!

It helped me to reframe my initial attempt as Anne Lamott's "shitty first draft." It took away the fear that my writing might be terrible because it didn't matter anymore. It might be terrible, but I could fix it later.

Give yourself permission to write whatever you want in that first draft with the knowledge that only you will see it.

Create the block of stone from which you will create your finished work

This metaphor might also help. Consider Michelangelo's famous statue of David, which stands in the Accademia Gallery in Florence, Italy. It is a perfection of a finished work of art, an iconic sculpture that draws people from all over the world hundreds of years after its creation.

Michelangelo said that he could see the finished sculpture in the marble. All he had to do was cut away the extraneous material to reveal it.

Imagine an enormous block of marble hewn straight from the quarry.

Michelangelo would have hacked at it with heavy tools at first to remove larger pieces, then used finer chisels, then ground and polished until, finally, the statue of David emerged, a creative vision in marble.

Now think about writing a novel.

We have to create the block of marble — the first draft — so we can then hack, chisel, grind, and polish in the editorial process until we reach our finished creative vision in words.

Have fun! Or at least find joy and satisfaction in the process

As writers, we often take ourselves way too seriously.

But why would you write if it was only going to be painful?

I spent thirteen years in a job I hated; every day featured tasks I found pointless, except as a way to pay the bills.

Of course, writing is a challenge. It's hard work, and it's tiring.

But you're making stuff up by choice. It's creative, it could even be… [shock horror] fun!

Consider the first draft as a form of creative play. You can mess around, no one will see it. Free your inner child and see what they come up with.

> "I believe that enjoying your work with all your heart is the only truly subversive position left to take as a creative person these days."
>
> —Elizabeth Gilbert, *Big Magic*

Questions:

- How will you approach the first draft? What attitude shift might help?

Resources:

- *Big Magic: Creative Living Beyond Fear* — Elizabeth Gilbert
- *Bird by Bird: Some Instructions on Writing and Life* — Anne Lamott
- *Succulent Wild Woman: Dancing with Your Wonder-full Self* — SARK

"The writing process alchemically alters me, leaving me transformed."

—bell hooks,
Remembered Rapture

4.2 How to write the first draft

> "Almost all good writing begins with terrible first efforts. You need to start somewhere."
>
> —*Anne Lamott, Bird by Bird*

When you haven't written a book before, you assume it's easy enough. This is why authors commonly hear things at parties like, 'Oh, yes, I'll write a novel someday when I have the time.' As if time is all you need.

I still find first drafts challenging after more than thirty books, but I have some specific processes and tools that help me get it done.

Schedule time blocks for writing — and only write in that time

Scheduling your writing time really is the secret to completing a novel. If you get your butt in the chair, or stand and dictate, for consistent periods of time, you *will* finish a draft.

Get out your calendar and schedule time for writing, as you would for any other important commitment.

If you can't block out hours of free time, schedule smaller chunks, or postpone other commitments until you're finished.

Turn up for that meeting with yourself and write.

It doesn't matter if the words aren't great. You can clean them up in the editing process, but you need to get black on white and finish that first draft in order to edit it into something useful later.

Don't do anything else during that time block. No email, no social media, no messaging. Just get words on the page.

> "Write at the edges of the day."
>
> —*Toni Morrison*

Find a location that will help you create

Our brains get used to specific locations for specific things. If you always watch TV from the couch, you'll sit down on it and automatically turn the TV on. If you use the home office for email or accounts, or if it's cluttered with children's projects, or unfinished DIY projects or artwork, you'll find it hard to write your novel in there.

Most of the time, I write in a local café. I get there when it opens and write for a few hours. I wear noise-cancelling headphones and listen to rain and thunderstorms on repeat. I drink one black coffee per hour, leaving once it gets busy so the café can use the table for higher-paying customers.

If I'm dictating, I book a room in a local co-working space and create there. Both options cost a little money, but the act of getting out of the house and committing to a different location can make all the difference in getting words on the page.

During the pandemic, I wrote in my home office, which was a challenge at first as I use the space for so many other things. In the end, I shifted my state by listening to different orchestral movie soundtracks, which changed the tone of my writing time compared to my admin and business work.

When we lived in London, I used to write in the London Library, and when I had a day job in Australia, I would write from 5:00 a.m. before work in the spare room of our house.

Find somewhere you can focus only on your novel without distractions.

Once you are in the location at the specified time,

make sure you won't be disturbed. Turn your phone to Do Not Disturb or airplane mode. Turn off social media and email. You can even use an app like Freedom to block internet access for a limited time. If you're working from home, put a sign on your door that you should only be disturbed in emergencies. If you are continually disrupted anyway, get out of the house next time.

Use timed writing sessions

Once you have scheduled your writing, use the time effectively. This might be heads down for the whole time or broken up by small breaks for coffee, stretching, or comfort stops. Some authors like to use the Pomodoro Technique — twenty-five minutes of writing, then a five-minute break — repeated several times per session.

I use Google Calendar to schedule time for writing and my Apple Watch reminds me to take a break if I haven't stood up for a while. I can usually do a couple of hours with mini breaks and then I need a longer walk. Writing for hours takes practice, so go slowly at first.

Setting a timer can help you focus more intensely on the writing period, then take a break. You'll achieve more than if you try to write for an hour or two with no scheduled breaks, especially if you haven't yet gained the stamina for long writing sessions.

When the timer starts, don't wait for inspiration. The Muse doesn't arrive when you sit around wishing she would. She turns up when you start creating, so get writing.

Find some way to make writing a habit. Don't leave it too long between writing sessions. Find ways to settle into your rhythm more quickly.

> "Be regular and orderly in your life, so that you may be violent and original on the page."
>
> —*Gustave Flaubert*

Use challenges, sprints, and community support

Some writers find it useful to write in a communal way, spurred on by the collective energy of a challenge.

You can find groups online — for example, #writingsprint on Twitter or #5amwritersclub if you're an early bird. Writershour.com offers an online group writing experience, and there are many other online options in every time zone.

You will also find groups of writers who meet at cafés or libraries on MeetUp or Eventbrite, so you will probably be able to find something to suit you. Or start your own writing group. Just remember to write and not chat!

There are also challenges like NaNoWriMo, National Novel Writing Month, which is every November. The challenge is to write 50,000 words of a first draft in a month, and there are all kinds of virtual and in-person events you can join.

I did NaNoWriMo in November 2009 and wrote the first 20,000 words of what eventually became *Stone of Fire*. It helped me break through my self-doubt and just get on with writing. Technically, I didn't 'win' as I only wrote 20,000 words, but that month kick-started my fiction career.

Writing groups

Some writers find groups work well for them, and others struggle with criticism or a mismatch in the type of writing style.

Some groups balance writing words with conversation and support, while others are more about a drink and a chat with creative friends.

When deciding if a writing group is right for you, make sure the members appreciate your chosen genre. Don't expect useful, positive feedback about your horror, epic fantasy, or romance novel in a group that focuses on literary fiction, or vice versa.

If you go to a writing group, assess how it's working for you over time. Is it a positive experience? Is it helping your writing? Do you leave excited about creating, or do you leave confused, depressed, and struggling to deal with criticism? Only you can decide what kind of group works for you, or if you need one at all. I've never been part of a writing group and have never felt the need for one, but I know plenty of authors who love them. It's up to you.

Write in any order

Don't try to write the first sentence of the first chapter first, unless you have such a detailed outline that it's ready to go.

You can jump around and write in any order — especially if you're a discovery writer.

You will find ideas for other scenes as you go, so note down those thoughts and carry on. You can always re-order everything later. You just want to get it all down in the first draft phase.

Track your progress

Writing a novel can be a daunting prospect, especially if the words are hard to produce and you manage little in some sessions.

But when you break it down, writing a novel is just a series of words arranged in sentences, gathered together into chapters and collected into book form. If you have managed a sentence, a paragraph, or a page, you have taken another step on the journey.

Tracking your progress can help you feel you're achieving something, however small. Some authors use spreadsheets to track time writing and/or number of words. Or you can just write them on a wall chart, or note them in an app.

I keep a day book by my desk where I write a few lines on what happened each day. When I'm writing a first draft, I add my word count and a colored sticker for each writing session. My inner creative child loves stickers!

Scrivener has a Project Targets section where you can set and track word count per session and it turns green if you achieve your goal. I also use colored flags, turning the chapters yellow when I have finished the first draft. I turn them blue after editing, and green when they are finished and ready to publish. This makes a manuscript more visually manageable, and if I can turn one flag yellow by the end of a writing session, I feel like I have won the day. More on writing tools in chapter 4.7.

Focus and shiny object syndrome

> "You must finish what you start."
>
> —Robert A. Heinlein, *Heinlein's Rules*

Writing is simple, but it's not easy.

There will always be distractions, and finishing a project has a lot to do with your ability to focus over a period of time and avoid shiny object syndrome.

"Ooh look, a new story idea! That is so cool, much more interesting than this old idea I'm working on over here. Why don't I just spend a bit of time on that new, shiny story and leave the old one in the corner? I'll go back to it later."

If you feel this urge and give into it every time, you will never finish your novel.

You will always have other ideas as you write. It's part of the creative process, and many of those ideas won't fit into the story you're currently writing.

It's a wonderful thing to have new ideas all the time, but if you keep following them in different directions, they will derail you.

So, if you're struck by a new shiny idea in the middle of your novel, write it down in a couple of sentences wherever you keep your idea lists, then turn back to your work in progress.

Beware trying to write multiple books at the same time, as you may not finish any of them. Some advanced writers manage this, but if you're just starting out, focus on one. Don't start another book if you haven't finished the one you've committed to.

How much do you want this?

If you're struggling to find the time to write, then revisit the reason you're writing. Does this novel *really* mean that much to you?

We all make time for the things we value. If you're not making time for writing, then it's not high enough on your list.

That's okay, because life is difficult enough without writing a novel! The only person who can decide whether it's worth the time is you.

My turning point came when I fully committed to

the writing path. I stuck at my consulting job for many years, thinking that it was just what I had to do to get by. It was only when I started crying at work most days, wondering what the hell I was doing with my life, that my motivation became significant enough to make a change.

I got up at 5:00 a.m. to write, learn the craft, and build my author platform. When I returned home after work, I didn't watch TV. I read books on writing, creative business, and online marketing. At the weekends, I ducked out of social arrangements in order to have a whole day to work on my writing. I made the time by giving up other things.

Writing is simple, but it's not easy. Getting black on white can sometimes seem like the hardest thing in the world, and yet your novel will be nothing without words on a page.

Getting them down takes time, and setting aside time takes discipline until we develop a creative habit. Even then, there are tough days.

Here's an excerpt from my journal in 2014:

> Today has been a difficult day. I procrastinated when I should have been writing. I emailed instead of creating things. I did busywork and

admin that didn't achieve much. I spent time on Twitter instead of writing. I bet Stephen King wouldn't behave like this. He would sit at his desk and write something new. Today I am a tired, disillusioned misery. But tomorrow I will be an author again. I promise.

The challenge to find writing time is a daily struggle, no matter where you are in your career, but ultimately, writers write, they don't just talk (or tweet or blog or Facebook or Instagram) about writing.

If you don't make time to work on your novel, you are the only one who suffers, as I did in the journal excerpt above.

You can find more tips in my book *Productivity for Writers*.

> "What people say they want and what they're willing to work their ass off to get are two different things."
>
> —Hugh MacLeod, *Evil Plans*

Questions:

- Have you scheduled time blocks for writing in your calendar, not just in your head? Have you actually written them down?
- Have you found a location where you can write without being disturbed?
- Have you found ways to stop yourself from being distracted when you write?
- Are you going to use timed writing sessions? How will you break these up?
- How will you track your progress through the book?
- How will you know when the first draft is finished?
- Do you suffer from shiny object syndrome? Do you have lots of unfinished projects on the go? How will you structure your time so you finish this book? How will you keep yourself focused and on track?
- How much do you want this? What will you say to yourself if you struggle with writing?

Resources:

- Google Calendar for scheduling time blocks: www.google.com/calendar

- BOSE QuietComfort noise-cancelling headphones. Pricey but worth it. I wear them every time I write now, even when dictating. My link: www.TheCreativePenn.com/silence

- Freedom app: www.freedom.to

- Scrivener software for organizing research, planning, writing and formatting — www.TheCreativePenn.com/scrivenersoftware

- *Evil Plans: Having Fun on the Road to World Domination* — Hugh MacLeod

- *Heinlein's Rules: Five Simple Business Rules for Writing* — Dean Wesley Smith

- *Productivity for Authors: Find Time to Write, Organize Your Author Life, and Decide What Really Matters* — Joanna Penn

4.3 Dictate your book

The word 'writing' is associated with hitting keys on a keyboard to make letters appear on a screen, or inscribing by hand onto paper. But the result is a mode of communication from one brain to another through the medium of words. Your voice can generate those words just as much as your fingers.

Famous dictating authors include John Milton (*Paradise Lost*), Dan Brown, Henry James, Barbara Cartland, and Winston Churchill. When Terry Pratchett, fantasy author of the Discworld series, developed Alzheimer's disease, he couldn't write anymore, so he moved to dictation in his final years.

Clearly, dictation can work for many writers across different genres, and it has become more popular for authors as technology makes it easier and faster. Why might you consider dictation?

Writing speed and stamina

Most people can speak faster than they write, so dictation is faster at getting words on the page than typing.

You have to know what you want to write before you speak, so it's more effective for plotters and outliners than for discovery writers. I've dictated at later stages of my novels, and used it more effectively for nonfiction, including the first draft of this book.

You will need to do a light edit to correct transcription issues each time, but if you want to get your first draft done faster, dictation can be effective.

Increased creativity

Some writers have a problem with perfectionism and critical voice in the first draft. They struggle to finish a book because they constantly edit what they write. If you dictate, you can bypass critical voice, get the first draft done, and edit later.

Health reasons

You can dictate standing up or walking, or even lying in bed, and many writers with health issues find dictation useful. Dictation can help ease or prevent pain now, and learning how to write with dictation can also future-proof your living as a writer in case of health problems later.

I started dictating when I developed pain in my wrists and forearms and used it to write some of the first drafts of my thrillers *Destroyer of Worlds* and *Map of Shadows*.

I eventually corrected the pain issues through changes to my health and fitness (which I wrote about in *The Healthy Writer*), and now I prefer to write in a local café, which is not so conducive to dictation. But I'm glad I learned the skill and I use it occasionally, just not for every book.

What's stopping you from dictating?

There are many reasons people resist dictation. I know them all because I've been through this journey!

The most common are:

- I'm used to typing. I don't have the right brain for dictation.
- I don't want to say the punctuation out loud. It will disrupt my flow.
- I have an accent which will make it difficult for the software to transcribe my words correctly.
- I write fantasy books with weird names that won't work for dictation.
- I don't know how to set it up technically.
- I can't spare the time to learn how to dictate.

Here's what I wrote in my journal on the first day I tried dictation before I'd even started.

> I'm very self-conscious. I'm worried that I won't be able to find the words. I'm so used to typing and creating through my fingers that doing it with my voice feels strange. But I learned to type with my fingers, so why can't I learn to type with my words? I just have to practice. Something will shift in my mind at some point, and it will just work.
>
> This should make me a healthier author, and also someone who writes faster. Authors who use dictation are writing incredibly fast. That's what I want. I want to write stories faster, as I have so many in my mind that I want to get into the world.

Here are thoughts from my journal *after* the first session:

> It felt like the words were really bad and the story clunky and poor. But actually, when the transcription was done, and I edited it, it wasn't as bad as I thought it would be. A classic case of critical voice. I need to ignore this when I'm dictating.

I thought I would find the punctuation difficult, but it was easier than expected. There are only a few commands you use regularly, and dialogue is the worst, but you get into a rhythm with that. It also gives you a pause between each speaker to consider what they might say next, so perhaps it is a blessing in disguise.

So whatever your reservations, give dictation a try and you might find the reality is easier than you think.

Different methods of dictation

There are two primary methods of dictation:

(1) Speech to text in real time

Dictate straight into a program or app, and adjust the words on the screen as you go. You may also be using voice commands to do other tasks — for example, to open email, send messages, and more.

(2) Dictate now, transcribe later

Use a recording device to record your words now and later have them transcribed. You can send them to a transcription service or use AI transcription or upload them into Dragon or another speech-to-text program.

I tried real-time speech-to-text and struggled with critical voice and a need to edit as the words appeared on the screen. So I switched to recording into a handheld device and uploaded it for transcription later.

I've tried different transcription options — Dragon Dictate on my Mac, Dragon Anywhere on the iPhone, Descript AI transcription, and Speechpad. com for human transcription. All have different levels of accuracy and cost, but all need at least a light edit to make sense of the entire transcription.

Speech-to-text technology is improving incredibly fast and will only continue to improve with the mainstream adoption of voice-first devices. Start with one variation based on the process you want to use, and your budget, and change as necessary once you discover what works for you.

Mobile apps and recording on the move

Since most people carry a phone anyway, it makes sense to use it for dictation. There are many apps. Some are free, some have subscriptions, and most sync with the cloud so you don't have to worry about losing your recordings.

Options include Dragon Anywhere, Dictation, Dictate Pro, and apps like Otter.ai, which use artificial intelligence to transcribe.

I also have a handheld Sony ICD-PX333 MP3 recording device which I sometimes use when out walking and dictating to conserve my phone battery.

The quality of your recordings on the move will be better if you use a microphone or headset. There are some with wind and noise-cancellation settings, with options improving all the time.

At-home options for computers

You can record straight into your computer using built-in options. On a Mac, look for the Start Dictation command in the Edit menu of most programs. On a PC, use the Speech Recognition tool. You can also dictate into Google Docs and other word processing tools.

You can also use premium software like Dragon, which you can train to recognize your specific speech patterns.

Again, the quality of the recording will improve if you use a microphone. I have a Blue Yeti, which I also use for podcasting.

Dictation tips from writers who use it

International bestselling and multi-award-winning author Kevin J. Anderson dictates all his books. He says,

> "The biggest advice that I would give for you and for other writers to get started with dictation is don't try to write that way. The best way to start is to do notes or brainstorming. Take your recorder and just go for a walk. It's almost like free association."

Kevin dictates while hiking in Colorado and then sends the files to a human transcriptionist every day. He shares more tips in his book *On Being a Dictator*.

Monica Leonelle, author of *Dictate your Book*, says,

> "Dragon thinks very differently than we do. We think in words. But Dragon thinks in phrases. So think about what you're going to say and then speak it with confidence. This makes the punctuation easier too."

This tip applies to any speech-to-text software. I dictate my text messages into my iPhone, and although it starts transcribing as I start speaking, it often changes the sentence once I have finished, so it reflects what I say more accurately by the end. The AI engine needs the whole context for the words to be correct.

Scott Baker, author of *The Writer's Guide to Training Your Dragon*, says,

> "Embrace dictation as a productivity tool. It's a weapon in your writing arsenal and your workflow. Don't treat it like it's something completely alien.
>
> We're familiar with the keyboard, but that isn't necessarily the best input method, anyway. Input methods keep changing. We've had the quill, and then we had the pen and then we had the typewriter and now we have the computer keyboard. In the last few years, we've had touch. I genuinely believe that the next big input method is voice.
>
> In the next 10 years, if you're not embracing voice, you will be behind in the same way as if you don't have a smartphone right now. You're missing out on a lot of technological help."

Questions:

- Why might you consider dictation? How might it help your writing?
- What's stopping you from dictating? How can you work through those issues in order to try it?
- What method of dictation might work for you?
- What tools do you need to get started?

Resources:

- *Dictate your Book: How to Write Your Book Faster, Better, and Smarter* — Monica Leonelle
- *Foolproof Dictation: A No-Nonsense System for Effective & Rewarding Dictation* — Christopher Downing
- *On Being A Dictator: Using Dictation To Be a Better Writer* — Kevin J. Anderson and Martin L. Shoemaker
- *The Writer's Guide to Training your Dragon: Using Speech Recognition Software to Dictate Your Book and Supercharge Your Writing Workflow* — Scott Baker

4.4 Write fast, cycle through, or write slow

Authors write in different ways, and there are different approaches to first drafts. Here are some options to consider.

Option 1: Write fast and rough

Write your first draft as fast as you can. Clear your schedule and produce words daily, or at least every couple of days, to keep your momentum going. This way, you stay in the world of the story. Everything is fresh in your mind, and you will be encouraged at how fast your manuscript grows.

Don't edit what you write as you go. Just get the words on the page.

Some writers call this a sprint. You can find authors on Twitter using #writerssprint if you want to join other people writing at the same time. Others call it binge writing, a term I like as it has that slightly naughty implication of ignoring everything else to focus on something you really enjoy!

This method might mean you have to do more in edits later, but to use the Michelangelo *David* metaphor, at least you will have your block of marble. You can shape it into a finished manuscript in the editorial process.

This is how some authors write a draft so quickly. They get their butts in the chair and set aside significant blocks of time.

Nora Roberts is a multi-award-winning, multi-best-selling author of over 200 novels across romance, fantasy, crime as J.D. Robb, and other genres. She is one of the best-loved and wealthiest authors in the world, and she is a prolific creator.

Nora explains how she writes on her blog:

> "I write every day… In the normal course of events, I work six to eight hours a day… I'm usually in work mode by 8. Sometimes before, sometimes later, that's just usual. I work. Stare into space, wonder WTF should happen next, look stuff up, and somehow by around 3 (sometimes earlier, sometimes later) I've actually written a decent chunk… Routine is my god."

Nora is a discovery writer. She doesn't outline, and she writes four or five books a year. Her blog is full of no-nonsense writing advice, so definitely check it out for more of her writing tips.

Many authors who write fast in the indie community are outliners and know what they want to achieve before they sit down to write or dictate. You will have to find the method that works best for you, but the main thing is to set aside bigger chunks of time to write. You cannot write a first draft quickly if you only have two hours a week to spare.

> "If your goal is to become a faster writer, the single most efficient change you can make isn't actually upping your daily word count, but eliminating the days where you are not writing."
>
> —Rachel Aaron, 2,000 to 10,000

Option 2: Write fast, cycle through

Another way is to write your words fast but then circle back each session, rereading and lightly editing what you wrote in the days before. This works well with dictation and also makes the editing process easier.

At the start of your writing session, circle back over the last scene and lightly edit, perhaps altering dialogue or adding depth, and then continue writing into new words for the session.

Your first draft will be tighter than the purely writing fast method above. In fact, some authors who write this way finish with a clean draft on the first pass.

Dean Wesley Smith explains this in *Writing into the Dark*.

> "I climb inside a character's head and get the emotions of the character about the setting around the character, and I type for two or three pages.
>
> 500 to 700 words or so.
>
> And I come to a halt.
>
> Every time, without fail. This is now a dug-in habit.
>
> I instantly jump out of the timeline of the story and cycle back to the first word and start through the story again.
>
> Sometimes I add in stuff, sometimes I take out, sometimes I just reread, scanning forward, fixing any mistakes I see…
>
> When I get back to the white space, I have some speed up and I power onward, usually another 500 or so words until I stop.
>
> Then I cycle back again to the beginning and do the same thing."

If you try this cycling method and find yourself stuck on editing, obsessing over typos and finding perfect metaphors, or getting depressed by how bad it is, then skip cycling and go back to the simple fast-drafting option above.

Option 3: Write slow

Some authors like to write more slowly and focus on making each sentence and paragraph and chapter the best it can be before moving forward.

This incorporates some form of editing into the writing process and results in fewer words per day, but perhaps more polished words in total, so the book will need less work in the editorial process. It can also be effective if you have an outline, as you already know what the book will be, so you can focus on expanding that outline into a full manuscript.

But beware. If you engage the critical editor's brain too early, you may pull your story apart before it's even come to life. It might bring up issues of perfectionism and you may end up writing so slowly that you don't ever finish. If this happens, go back to the first option of getting that first draft done as fast as possible.

Questions:

- Which of these methods suits you the best? Have you tried other options?

Resources:

- "Here's how I work," Nora Roberts's blog — fallintothestory.com/heres-how-i-work/

- *Writing into the Dark: How to Write a Novel without an Outline* — Dean Wesley Smith

- *2,000 to 10,000: Writing Faster, Writing Better, and Writing More of What You Love* — Rachel Aaron

- *5,000 Words Per Hour: Write Faster, Write Smarter* — Chris Fox

4.5 Writer's block

> "If you get stuck, get away from your desk. Take a walk, take a bath, go to sleep, make a pie, draw, listen to music, meditate, exercise; whatever you do, don't just stick there scowling at the problem."
>
> *—Hilary Mantel*

Most writers struggle with getting words on the page at some point. But writer's block is not one monolithic thing, and it does not have one cause or one cure. The term encompasses issues with different root causes and varying solutions.

Here are some reasons you might feel blocked.

You don't know how to write a novel

If you don't know *how* to write a book, you can end up flailing around and wasting time, frustrated because you're not getting anywhere.

Hopefully, this book will help you.

If you're still struggling, go back to the first principles: schedule timed writing sessions, get your butt in the chair, and figure it out along the way.

You're trying to write the wrong kind of book

If you try to write something you think you 'should' write because of the expectations of others, or a need for validation by other people, then you may struggle more than you need to.

I had this kind of block before writing my first novel. I thought the only book I should attempt to write was something literary and prize-winning, something that might attract literary acclaim. Those were the books I studied at school and university, those were the books praised by the media. But I didn't really have any ideas for that kind of novel and, to be honest, a lot of them bored me.

But then I realized that the books I craved as a reader were the thrillers that helped me escape the job I hated. I read on the commuter train in the morning; I read with my sushi at lunch (if I could get away from my desk); I read on the train home again, in bed before sleeping, and in the hammock at the weekend. I read thrillers and escapist fiction every moment I could.

I decided to write an international thriller based around my fascination with religion and aim it at 'commuter Jo.' That shift freed me from my block and my writing took off.

So, don't worry. You don't need to write an 'important' book that becomes a literary classic and stands the test of time. Be honest with yourself. Write something you want to read.

You might also have ambitions that go beyond what you can write at this point, either with the length of the book or the scope. If you want to write a Tolkien-esque *Lord of the Rings*–style epic fantasy eventually, perhaps it's best to start with something simple, something more like *The Hobbit*? You can work up to that magnum opus later once you have more experience.

You haven't filled the creative well

> "The word block suggests that you are constipated or stuck, when the truth is that you're empty."
>
> —Anne Lamott, *Bird by Bird*

You cannot create from an empty mind. You have to fill it somehow. Research, read, watch, travel, talk to people, do whatever you need to, but fill your mind with the raw material it can use to create your story.

I struggled to write fiction during the pandemic because my story ideas come from places I visit.

I need external input in order to create. Since I couldn't travel far at the time, I walked The Pilgrim's Way from London to Canterbury, and finally found inspiration for *Tomb of Relics* in the cathedral. I also wrote my short story *Blood, Sweat, and Flame* based on *Blown Away*, a series on Netflix about glassblowing.

You might find inspiration in different ways, but if you're struggling, get away from the blank page and fill your creative well, whatever that means to you.

You're trying to create in a way that is wrong for your personality or lifestyle

Sometimes we feel blocked because we try to force ourselves to create in a way that just doesn't fit with who we are.

If you're trying to outline and it's not working, try discovery writing.

If you're trying to write every day, stop for a week until the energy builds up and you need to binge write all the stuff in your brain onto the page.

If you're trying to write early in the morning at your kitchen table and you're distracted, try dictating on your phone while walking at lunchtime.

If you can't carve out an hour because you have a busy family and work life, try writing in fifteen minute blocks instead.

If you're feeling guilty because you're not writing — then consider why. Perhaps it's just not the right time in your life.

I know writers who have young children, elderly parents, a busy job, and health issues, and they feel guilty about not writing. But sometimes, life is just too much and writing can wait. You might not be blocked, you might just be overloaded.

You didn't realize that writing a novel was this hard

Writing a novel is a challenge. It's much harder than you expect it to be when you start out, so at some point, you will have to face the difficulty of knuckling down and doing the work.

People who haven't written a book before expect it to be a simple process to turn thoughts into words on a page. But it's tiring, and it takes stamina that you need to build up over time.

Some days you feel you're in flow and everything is amazing.

The next day, each sentence is a grind.

But that's not a block — it's the creative process.

Sometimes you just need a break.

If I'm stuck in the middle of a chapter, or just feeling over it, I go for a walk. Sometimes, if I've been working on something for an extended period of weeks or months, I need a longer break. A few days or weeks away from the manuscript, and you'll come back to the page renewed.

Fear of failure, fear of judgment, self-doubt, and other mindset issues

All these things will come up during the writing process and you can either choose to let them stop you, or you can spend some time wallowing, write in your journal about how hard it all is, and then get back to writing.

> For more on the mindset side of the creative life, check out my book *The Successful Author Mindset: A Handbook for Surviving the Writer's Journey.*

How much do you want this?

> "Brick walls are there to stop the people who don't want it badly enough."
>
> —*Randy Pausch, The Last Lecture*

If you're feeling blocked, but you are committed to writing this novel, then you need to figure out the problem and deal with it.

There will always be challenges. Your job is to overcome them and finish this book.

I love being a fiction author. I am so proud of my creative body of work. I can hold my books in my hands and say, "I made these!"

Writing that first novel changed my life, and I want that for you.

You *will* have brick walls along the way. Only you can smash through them.

Questions:

- If you're struggling with your writing, can you identify the reason behind the block?
- How can you deal with the block and still achieve your goal of writing a book? What

practical steps will you take to move your project forward and still look after yourself?

Resources:

- *Bird by Bird: Some Instructions on Writing and Life* — Anne Lamott

- *Conquering Writer's Block and Summoning Inspiration: Learn to Nurture a Lifestyle of Creativity* — K.M. Weiland

- *On Writing: A Memoir of the Craft* — Stephen King

- *The Last Lecture: Lessons in Living* — Randy Pausch

- *The Successful Author Mindset: A Handbook for Surviving the Writer's Journey* — Joanna Penn

- Interview on how to banish writer's block with K.M. Weiland on The Creative Penn Podcast: www.TheCreativePenn.com/weiland

- "Hilary Mantel's rules for writers," *The Guardian*, 22 Feb 2010 — www.theguardian.com/books/2010/feb/22/hilary-mantel-rules-for-writers

4.6 Writing tools and software

Some authors write by hand on paper, some dictate, some use a laptop or a phone to get the words down, but at some point, you need your manuscript in electronic format on a computer file.

Software won't write a book for you, but it can definitely help with organizing your ideas, managing your writing, and structuring your novel. Here are some tools that might help.

MS Word/Pages/Google Docs

Many writers use basic word processing options for their manuscripts. It doesn't have to be complicated!

Turn off formatting options so you don't get distracted by typos and grammar in the first draft.

Consider creating a document per scene or chapter, rather than just one long document, since it can become unwieldy and you might change the order of things later in the editing process.

Scrivener

I used MS Word for my first novel, but then I discovered Scrivener. I've used it for every book since then, both fiction and nonfiction, including this one.

As a discovery writer, I write out of order, and Scrivener makes it easy to write my scenes, add placeholders for things to write later, and drag and drop things around toward the end of the process.

Once I have a rough draft, I use the Inspector pane to make sure I've achieved my goals for each scene. Is there a cliff-hanger that makes the reader want to turn the page? What are some of the open questions I need to answer later?

I also use Project and Session Targets, so I can track word count per session. It turns green when you reach your goal, which helps with motivation.

You can find Scrivener at:

www.TheCreativePenn.com/scrivenersoftware

For a walk-through of how I use Scrivener, check out my tutorial:

www.TheCreativePenn.com/scrivenertutorial

Plotting software

You can use Scrivener for plotting and outlining. It has a corkboard view and other tools that make it easy to add detail. But there are other software options if you love outlining and want to plot. I haven't used any of these, but they are recommended by others in the writing community.

Plottr.com helps you add and arrange scenes, organize your timeline, keep a story bible up to date, and automate your outline. You can even use one of their structure templates to kick-start your story.

PlotFactory.com is a collaborative story planner that helps you organize your story universe, create rich characters, and generate plot outlines.

Granthika.co helps manage story elements and narrative structure, keeping track of people, places, things, and events. The award-winning author of *Sacred Games*, Vikram Chandra, who writes sprawling novels, created it when he couldn't find software that worked for his fiction needs.

These software tools should help you write a novel, not procrastinate by filling everything in for months on end! Make sure you spend more time writing than playing with software.

AI writing tools

Artificial intelligence underpins much of the modern writer's life, from powering Google search to improving editing software, and when the book is finished, it drives discoverability and marketing on the major online stores.

You can also use AI tools in the creation process — but, of course, I recommend using them in an ethical manner.

I sometimes use Sudowrite as a creative collaborative tool that provides all kinds of off-the-wall ideas. Sudowrite can help you brainstorm ideas, create characters and twists, expand your descriptions, experiment with different styles, and more.

You can use it to generate first-draft words from a prompt, but personally, I prefer to write my own stories in my voice and use Sudowrite more for idea generation and help with sensory description.

If you use text generation, make sure you run your manuscript through a plagiarism checker, as covered in chapter 5.5 on editing tools.

There are other AI-powered writing tools, but nothing I have found to be as useful as Sudowrite for fiction writers.

You can find Sudowrite at:

www.TheCreativePenn.com/sudowrite

For a walk-through of how I use Sudowrite, check out my tutorial:

www.TheCreativePenn.com/sudowritetutorial

Back up your manuscript every time you write

This might seem obvious, but I frequently hear from authors who have lost hours or days of writing, sometimes even whole manuscripts, because something technical went wrong.

Make sure this doesn't happen to you.

I write in Scrivener, but the same applies if you write in any kind of online or computer-based software. At the end of every writing session, I export my draft to .docx and save it as a new file in my Draft folder on my laptop.

I date every draft, so I end up with lots of documents within the folder, each representing the progress of the book, for example, Desecration120422.docx, Desecration130422.docx, and so on.

The Draft folder is automatically backed up on

Dropbox in the cloud. I also email the file to myself every time. I do this for every writing session, and sometimes twice a day if I have two separate sessions.

This might seem a little over-the-top, but it's like having insurance. If you have it, chances are you never have to use it. If you don't have it, and something happens, you end up regretting it.

Questions:

- What tools do you use for writing? What are the pros and cons of them?
- What other tools might be worth trying and why?

Resources:

- Dropbox — www.TheCreativePenn.com/dropbox
- Granthika — www.granthika.co
- PlotFactory — www.PlotFactory.com
- Plottr — www.plottr.com
- Scrivener — www.TheCreativePenn.com/scrivenersoftware
- Scrivener tutorial — www.TheCreativePenn.com/scrivenertutorial
- Sudowrite — www.TheCreativePenn.com/sudowrite
- Sudowrite tutorial — www.TheCreativePenn.com/sudowritetutorial
- Interviews and resources on AI writing — www.TheCreativePenn.com/future

4.7 When is the first draft finished?

> "I hate writing, I love having written."
>
> —*Dorothy Parker*

I consider a first draft finished when it is a coherent story end-to-end without things like [insert action scene] or [where is the dog?] or [add more setting detail] or [zzzz, come back to this later].

To use the Michelangelo metaphor, I have created my block of marble and the finished story is inside, waiting to be released.

The story is not perfect and I won't show it to anyone, but it is coherent with a beginning, a middle, and an end. I have answered the main story questions, the character has transformed in some way, the plot has concluded, and it feels complete. I've also organized the scenes into chapters so the novel progresses in a linear fashion and I can read it from start to finish.

I use flags in Scrivener to mark each chapter with a yellow flag. When all the flags are yellow, I export from Scrivener to Word and save that version with the date as usual.

I print the manuscript ready for editing with two pages per A4 page, so it is laid out like a 'real' book. I staple the pages together in blocks of around twenty and then put the manuscript in a folder on my desk, ready for editing.

You don't have to print it out, but do something that shows your draft is finished and you're moving onto the next stage.

Celebrate this milestone

Take a moment to step back and appreciate what you have achieved. A first draft is a tremendous step toward finishing a novel. Non-writers won't understand what this means, but I do — so congratulations!

I always feel a tremendous feeling of satisfaction when I finish the first draft. I know there's a way to go before I have a completed novel, but I've certainly climbed a lot of the mountain. Time for a gin and tonic or two!

How long does it take to write the first draft?

It's impossible to say because there are so many variables — how developed your story is, your experience, the genre, the length of the book, and how much time you set aside for writing.

Many authors talk about the years it took to write the first novel, but writing often speeds up once you know how the process works, and if you have a deadline, whether contractual or self-imposed, you'll have more boundaries on your time.

You can estimate if you set a timeline and schedule your writing blocks accordingly. Make some assumptions and adjust along the way.

Allow time for research, thinking, planning, plotting, and outlining, then decide on a specific day to start writing the draft.

If you write 1,000 words per session, and you're aiming for a 70,000 word novel, that will be 70 writing sessions of first-draft material.

If you set aside four writing sessions per week, it will take around eighteen weeks, or four to five months, to write that first draft.

You can speed it up by allotting more time, or slow it down if you need more time to meander along the way.

For my first novel, I enrolled in a Year of the Novel course at a local library. It gave me the structure and accountability I needed to ensure I finished the draft alongside working a day job, learning the craft, and building my author business along the way.

It took around nine months to write the first draft in the early mornings before work, evenings, and weekends, then I went through an editorial process. In the end, it took about sixteen months to go from idea to book and, since then, I have improved my process and writing speed.

Remember Parkinson's Law

Parkinson's Law notes that "work expands so as to fill the time available for its completion."

If your goal is to finish your novel, set a deadline and schedule your writing time accordingly, otherwise you could spend years, decades, or even the rest of your life working on it.

Questions:

- What is a finished first draft? How will you know when you have achieved it?

- How will you celebrate the significant milestone of a finished first draft?

- How will you make sure that you are not still writing this novel on your deathbed? Have you set a deadline and worked out your writing schedule?

Part 5:
The Editing Process

5.1 Overview of the editing process

"Books aren't written. They're rewritten."

—*Michael Crichton*

Thomas Hardy's *Tess of the d'Urbervilles* is a classic of English literature. I studied it at school and the scene at Stonehenge still haunts me. Hardy's *Jude the Obscure* influenced my decision to go to university in Oxford, a city Hardy called Christminster. His novels are still held in great esteem, which is why it's so wonderful to see his hand-edited pages in the British Library in London, displayed in the Treasures collection. You can visit them in person or view them online.

While his handwriting is a scrawl, it's evident from the pages just how much editing Hardy did on this version of the manuscript. There are lines struck through, whole paragraphs crossed out, arrows moving sections around, words and sentences rewritten, and comments in the margins. Even the title is changed from *A Daughter of the D'Urbervilles* to *Tess of the D'Urbervilles* as we know it today.

Those edited pages gave me hope when I saw them for the first time as a new fiction author. Not that I thought I could write a classic of English literature, but that I could learn to edit my way to a better story.

There are several stages in the editing process, which I'll outline here and then expand on in subsequent chapters. As you progress in your craft, you won't need every stage every time, so assess with each book what kind of editing you need along the way.

Self-editing

The self-editing stage is your chance to improve your manuscript before anyone else sees it. For some authors, this stage might mean rewriting the entire draft. For others, it involves restructuring, adding or deleting scenes, doing line edits, and more.

Developmental or structural edit

An editor reads your manuscript and gives feedback on specific aspects, character, plot, story structure, and anything else pertinent to improving the novel. It is sometimes described as a manuscript critique.

You will receive a report, usually ten to fifteen pages, with notes on your novel, which you can then use in another round of self-editing.

While this is not always necessary, it can be a valuable step and something I appreciated particularly for my first novel when I had so much to learn.

Copyediting and line editing

This is the classic 'red pen' edit where you can expect comments and changes all over your manuscript. This edit focuses on anything that enhances the writing quality, including word choice and phrasing issues, as well as grammar, and more.

Some editors split this edit into two, and there are differences between what this edit is called between countries. For some editors, a copyedit includes only attention to grammar and correctness, while a line edit focuses on improving and elevating sentences. Be clear about your expectations and that of your editor upfront.

You will usually receive an MS Word document with Track Changes on as well as a style guide or style sheet and other notes, which you can then use to make revisions during another self-edit.

This is the most expensive part of the process, as editors usually charge per 1,000 words based on the type of edit you want. If you need to cut your story down by 20K, then do it *before* you send your manuscript for a line edit!

Beta readers, specialist readers, and/or sensitivity readers

Some authors use different types of readers as part of their editing process.

Beta readers are often part of the author's community and are certainly fans of the genre. They read to help the author pick up any issues pre-publication.

Specialist readers are those with knowledge about a topic included in the story. For example, a vulcanologist read specific chapters of *Risen Gods* to check that the details about volcanic eruptions were correct.

Sensitivity readers check for stereotypes, biases, problematic language, and other diversity issues.

You will usually receive comments or an email with page numbers or chapter numbers, or sometimes an MS Word document with Track Changes, which you then use to make revisions.

Many readers provide services for the love of helping their favorite author with a novel and a mention in the acknowledgments, but there are some paid services for specialist and sensitivity readers.

Proofreading

Proofreading is the final check of the manuscript pre-publication for any typos or issues that might have been introduced in the editorial process. For print books, this can include a review of the print proof with formatting.

You should only fix the last tiny changes at this point. Don't make any major changes this close to publication or you may introduce entirely new errors.

Do you need an editor if you intend to get an agent and a traditional publisher?

You will go through an editorial process with your agent and publisher. But if you want the best chance of getting to that stage in the first place, it might also be worth working with an editor before you submit your manuscript to an agent. Look for an editor who will help you with your query letter and synopsis as part of their edit.

Questions:

- What types of editing might you consider for your manuscript?

Resources:

- British Library Collection Manuscript of *Tess of the d'Urbervilles* by Thomas Hardy — www.TheCreativePenn.com/tess

5.2 Self-editing

I love this part of the process! My self-edit is where I wrangle the chaos of the first draft into something worth reading. I have my block of marble and now I can shape it into my sculpture.

The mindset shift from writer to editor, from author to reader

In the idea, planning, discovery, and first-draft writing phase, it's all about you, the writer.

You turn the ideas in your head into words that you understand, characters that come alive for you, and a plot that you're engaged with. In that first rush of creativity, you can banish critical voice and ignore any nagging doubts.

But now you need to switch heads.

That's how I prefer to think about it, but you might consider it as changing hats or changing jobs. Anything to help you move from the creative, anything goes, first-draft writer to the more critical editor.

There is one overriding consideration in this shift. As Jeffery Deaver says, "The reader is god."

With the editing process, you need to turn your story from something you understand into something a reader will enjoy.

Writing is telepathy. It connects minds across time and space.

You are reading these words and the meaning flows from my brain into your brain — but only if I craft the book well enough. The same is true of your novel.

Yes, of course, you want to double down on your creative choices and make sure you achieve everything you want to with your story. But you also need to keep the reader in mind as you edit because the book is ultimately for them.

Will your story have the desired effect on the reader?

What might help improve their experience?

How can you make sure that they are not bored or confused or jolted out of the story?

What will make them read on and, at the end, close the novel with a sigh of satisfaction?

My self-editing process

At the end of the first draft, I print out my manuscript with two pages to each A4 page, so it looks more like a book. I put it in a folder and leave it to rest. You need fresh eyes for your edit and this 'resting' gives you some emotional distance.

In *On Writing*, Stephen King suggests leaving a manuscript to rest for at least six weeks. While that is a great idea if you have the time, most authors work to deadline, whether externally set or their own timetable.

Many authors — including me — are also impatient! I love this first self-edit, and as I'm still crafting the story as a discovery writer, I usually rest the manuscript for a week or two.

I schedule blocks of time for editing in my Google calendar and (when not in pandemic times) I go to a café when it opens first thing in the morning. I put on my BOSE noise-cancelling headphones and edit by hand with a black ballpoint pen from page one to the end.

I usually manage ten to twenty pages per editing session of a couple of hours each, but it will depend on the amount of restructuring I need to do.

I scribble notes in the margins, draw arrows to move paragraphs around, write extra material on the back of pages, or add where I need to write more later. I change words, rewrite and delete lines, and pick up any issues around lack of sensory detail, character problems, and more.

You can see an example of a page at:

www.TheCreativePenn.com/handedit

Some pages end up a mass of black; others are relatively clean. But in this first hand edit, no page goes untouched as I hone my manuscript into something closer to my creative goal.

You can edit on a computer or a tablet, or whatever else works for you, but at least change the font or the spacing, or something to make it a different experience to reading the first draft.

Most writers have a tendency to either overwrite or underwrite, and so will either need to cut words or add words at this stage. I'm in the latter camp so I usually have to add scenes or deepen characters or theme at this point.

Once I have hand-edited the whole manuscript end-to-end, I make the changes in my Scrivener project. I change the color of the flags along the way and, as ever, I back up the session.

When all the changes have been made, I print the complete manuscript again, and read end-to-end and edit as before. This time, it's usually a lot cleaner and there may only be a few things to fix in each chapter.

Once I'm finished, I'll update the Scrivener project once more and then decide whether it needs a third pass. Mostly, two full end-to-end hand edits are enough for me these days, but sometimes I'll do a third or go through specific chapters one more time.

This messy editing process is fun for me and it's hugely satisfying to see my story come to life.

What to focus on in the self-edit

Some authors will go through the manuscript multiple times, focusing on different elements with each pass using the aspects covered in Part 3 and Part 4. For example, they'll do an edit based on character and dialogue, followed by another pass for plot, then theme, and so on.

Personally, I try to keep the reader in mind and focus on the story as a coherent whole. That's just how my mind works.

I jump from fixing a plot issue to deepening a character to adding foreshadowing and so on as I read and edit. I'm confident that my editor will find a lot of the smaller things that I might miss, so I concentrate on trying to achieve my creative vision with the story.

You will find your own way of figuring out your process. It's much better to jump in and have a go at editing rather than trying to work out the best way before you have something to work through.

Lost the plot? Try reverse outlining

If you're a discovery writer like me and you're struggling with the edit and you feel you have lost the plot (which definitely happens sometimes!) then consider a reverse outline as part of your editorial process.

Go through the manuscript and write a few lines per scene. Include character, plot points, conflict, setting, open questions and hooks, and any other notes.

This will help you step back and hopefully see the entire story from a high level. Then you can dive back into rewriting each chapter.

Read the book out loud or use a text-to-speech reader to do it for you

Many authors read their book aloud end-to-end, which is a helpful step once you've been through any major rewrites.

There are also plenty of text-to-speech tools that can help, for example, Natural Reader or Speechify, and some are built into devices or applications. MS Word includes a Read Aloud tool in the Review tab. This will also help you edit for audio as you'll hear issues you can't see on the page.

Editing for audio

Audiobooks are a huge growth market and many readers will listen to your book rather than read it, so it's a good idea to consider editing with audio in mind at this stage. Here are some tips.

Watch out for repeated sounds.

The editorial process will usually catch repeated written words, but similar sounding words can hit the same audio note in narration. You might not notice them in the text, as they are spelled differently. The words 'you,' 'blue,' 'tattoo,' and 'interview' all start and end with different letters. They look different on the page, but they strike the same audio note when read aloud.

In the same way, repetition can work if you have a point to make, but sometimes it jars the listener if it is overused.

A classic recommendation for writing dialogue is to use 'said' with a character name rather than other words like 'uttered' or 'pronounced.' This is because 'said' disappears for the reader on the written page. But with audio, the repetition of a word is highly noticeable, and repeated sounds can dominate a passage.

Rewrite with synonyms for 'said,' or use action to make it clear who the speaker is without resorting to dialogue tags, as described in chapter 3.5.

Contractions — or the lack of them — can also become more obvious in audio.

"I am not going to the park," might be spoken as "I'm not going to the park." When we type dialogue, it is often more formal than the way someone speaks, so check if you can contract it in your edit.

Accents can be an issue with fiction narration.

There are plenty of narrators who do a 'straight read,' but if there are accents within dialogue, make it clear where the character comes from. Make sure the narrator knows about the accent choice upfront, otherwise you might not like it in the finished audio. Remember my friend whose novel had an Irish character narrated like a comedy leprechaun instead of the soft lilt she had in mind?

Don't confuse the reader.

If you have a lot of characters appearing in a chapter and no clear character tags, you might lose the listener in the detail.

When reading on paper or a screen, your reader can quickly flick back and see that George was the butler and Angus was the dog, but that's harder to do when listening to an audiobook. Make sure it's clear who is who. You may have to remind listeners occasionally by adding character tags. For example, 'Angus ran alongside the canal' could become 'Angus, the golden cocker spaniel, ran alongside the canal.'

> For more on audiobooks, check out my book, *Audio for Authors: Audiobooks, Podcasting and Voice Technologies*.

How many drafts do you need?

The word 'draft' means different things to different authors. Some only apply this term to a complete rewrite end-to-end, while others will shift paragraphs around, change some lines, add a new scene, and call that a new draft.

Nora Roberts said in a blog post on her writing craft,

> "I work on a three-draft method. This works for me. It's not the right way/wrong way. There is no right or wrong for a process that works for any individual writer. Anyone who claims there is only one way, or that's the wrong way, is a stupid, arrogant bullshitter. That's my considered opinion."

I love Nora's no-nonsense approach and she is right that there is no single correct process. You have to find your own. But beware of comparing what you call a draft to what another writer calls a draft. It may be something completely different.

Use editing software

Once I've finished my hand edits and updated the Scrivener project, I use ProWritingAid on the manuscript. It integrates with Scrivener, so I open my project and go through each chapter.

ProWritingAid picks up passive voice, repetitive words, commas and typos, suggests rephrasing, and even picks up culturally problematic language.

Yes, these are the type of things that an editor will pick up, but I want to hand over a manuscript that is as clean as possible so my editor can focus on other issues. I don't make all the suggested changes, but it certainly helps improve my writing, and I learn as I go through. You can even create your own style guide so you spell things the same way throughout.

This is also a good chance to check typos according to the version of English you want to use (or any other language). I'm English and based in the UK, but when I published my first novel, I received complaints about typos from my readers, who were mainly in the USA. These were not typos, they were just British spelling!

I decided to use US English in my books because US readers complain about UK spelling, but non-US readers will rarely complain about US spelling because they are used to it. You can set ProWritingAid to the type of English you want to use, and if you specify this later, your editor can pick up on word usage rather than typos, for example, using the term 'flashlight' instead of 'torch.'

You can find ProWritingAid at:

www.TheCreativePenn.com/prowritingaid

You can find my tutorial on how to use ProWritingAid at www.TheCreativePenn.com/prowritingaidtutorial

When is your self-edit finished?

You will be utterly sick of your manuscript by the end of the self-editing process.

You have read your words so many times you can't see them clearly anymore. You are so over the whole thing that you want to forget the book altogether. If you don't feel this way, you probably haven't self-edited enough!

When you really feel you can't do any more, it's time to work with a professional editor.

If you are putting off the end of self-editing, then remember that nothing is ever perfect. You can edit forever if you keep obsessing over changes and going over and over the same material. If your self-edit goes on too long, consider whether perfectionism is holding you back. Set a completion date and hold yourself to it.

Questions:

- Have you set aside time for your self-editing process? Have you printed out the manuscript or created a new version with a different font so it looks different to the original?

- Have you shifted your mindset from writer to editor? Do you know what you want the reader's experience to be? How will you keep them in mind as you edit?

- How does your self-editing process work? What tools can you use?

- Is the reader's journey through the book as clear and easy as possible?

- Have you achieved your creative goal for the story? (Or at least made it as far as you can at this point?)

- How will you know when the self-edit is finished? How can you balance doing the best you can with avoiding perfectionism?

- Have you taken this self-editing process as far as you can? Are you ready to work with a professional editor?

Resources:

- "Here's how I work," Nora Roberts's blog — fallintothestory.com/heres-how-i-work/

- *Audio for Authors: Audiobooks, Podcasting and Voice Technologies* — Joanna Penn

- ProWritingAid — www.TheCreativePenn.com/prowritingaid

- Tutorial on how to use ProWritingAid — www.TheCreativePenn.com/prowritingaid-tutorial

- *Self-Editing for Fiction Writers: How to Edit Yourself into Print* — Renni Browne and Dave King

- *Intuitive Editing: A Creative and Practical Guide to Revising Your Manuscript* — Tiffany Yates Martin

- *The Novel Editing Workbook: 105 Tricks and Tips for Revising Your Manuscript* — Kris Spisak

"Brick walls are there to stop the people who don't want it badly enough."

—Randy Pausch, The Last Lecture

5.3 How to find and work with a professional editor

If you want your book to be the best it can be, then working with a professional editor is the next step.

An editor's job is to take your manuscript and help you improve it through structural changes and story development, line edits, suggestions for new material or sentence refinement, and so much more. Different kinds of editors can help you in different ways from constructing the overarching story to eliminating the final typo.

In my experience, good professional editors are well worth the investment as they help improve your book and your craft, especially in the initial stages of your writing journey. They have read so many early-stage manuscripts that they understand the most common problems and know how to help you fix them.

Some experienced authors only use proofreaders for their novels, but personally, I still work with a professional editor on every book and I learn something every time. I am a super-fan of editors!

How to find a professional editor

Consolidation in the traditional publishing industry over the last decade has resulted in many more editors working as freelancers, so authors have a wealth of professionals available for hire in every genre.

You can find lists of approved editors through author organizations. The Alliance of Independent Authors has a list of Partner Members, many of whom are editors. You can also use author marketplace Reedsy.

Many editors use content marketing to find clients — for example, blogging about editing tips, writing books on editing, or appearing on podcasts. I have had lots of editors on The Creative Penn Podcast over the years, so you can listen and see if they resonate with you.

Most authors credit their editors and proofreaders in the acknowledgments of their books, and many authors happily share recommendations on social media in various author communities. If you enjoy a certain novel, it might be worth reaching out to that editor, as you know they are a specialist in the genre.

Check out my list of editors at:

www.TheCreativePenn.com/editors

How to assess whether an editor is right for you

I frequently get emails from writers asking me to recommend an editor for their book.

But finding an editor is like dating.

You have to do it for yourself, and it's likely that you will try a few before you find your perfect match. You may also change editors over your writing life as your craft develops and your needs shift, and that's completely normal too.

Make sure the editor has experience in and enjoys your genre. You don't want a literary historical fiction editor working on your YA paranormal romance or your hard sci-fi adventure.

Ensure that the editor has testimonials from happy clients, and check directly with a named author if you have doubts.

Some editors will offer a sample edit for one chapter. This helps both parties decide whether working together is appropriate. The editor can assess what level your manuscript is at, and you can decide whether their editorial style is right for you.

How to work with an editor

When you engage an editor, you will receive a contract with a timeline and a price for the work.

You agree to deliver the manuscript on a particular date and will usually pay a deposit, especially if this is the first time you're working together. The editor agrees to deliver the edits back on a certain date and also to keep your manuscript in confidence.

You can avoid issues later by communicating expectations up front, so if you have questions about the editing process, ask before you sign a contract.

Many editors are booked months in advance, so once you know your schedule, contact them early and book a slot. Update them if your timings change. Most allow minor slippage, but since editors plan their work around contractual dates, it's important to be timely with delivery. As a discovery writer, I only book my editor when I am sure of my dates.

Submit your manuscript and, once the edit is complete, you will receive whatever has been agreed. That might be a structural report, line edit, or proofread manuscript, along with a style sheet. It's usually in the form of an MS Word document by email.

Some editors may offer a call to discuss, but I have never spoken to an editor as part of my process. It has never been necessary. It's all about the words on the page. If you want a call and it is not specified, then include it in the contract up front along with anything else you're concerned about.

I consider my editors to be an important part of my team. They help me turn my manuscripts into books that readers love, and I rely on them as part of my business. This is a two-way relationship, and you need to behave as professionally as the editor should. If you find an editor you love working with, pay them quickly and respect their time, and you will hopefully have a long-term business relationship that benefits you both.

How does it feel to go through an edit?

It's probably going to hurt, especially in the beginning, when your craft is in its early stages. You need fresh eyes on your work, especially at the beginning of your author career. You need feedback to improve.

When I received notes back on my structural edit for my first novel, I didn't open the email for ten days. I was so scared of what it would say because my novel meant so much to me, and yet I knew it had problems. Of course it did, it was my first novel! So I let the email sit in my inbox until I was ready to face it, and like many things, the fear was worse than the actual event.

Even many years and many books later, I still don't open emails from my editor until I am mentally ready to face criticism.

Because that's what it feels like.

It is not the editor's job to pat you on the back and say, 'Well done, this is perfect.'

Their job is to help you make it the best book it can be. They are experts and have honed their advice over many manuscripts, so they can spot an issue a mile off.

When you receive that email from your editor, particularly if it's your first book, make sure you are well rested and in a positive frame of mind. Set aside a good amount of time and read through the comments and the manuscript as a whole.

If you have an emotional reaction, *do not* email back immediately!

Let the feedback sit with you for a few days, and you will find it easier to see what might need to change.

Once you're ready, go through the manuscript and work through each change. Don't just click Accept All on the Track Changes version for a line edit. This takes time, but it's well worth it because you will learn with every step and you'll be able to spot your common issues in the future, and hopefully fix them next time. You also need to examine every suggestion to see if you want to make the change.

Do you need to make every change that an editor suggests?

No, you don't. You are the author, so your creative vision is the most important thing. But try to get some distance and assess whether your response truly serves the book, or if it is just an emotional response. Remember what Jeffery Deaver said: "The reader is god."

Consider each editorial suggestion on its own merit. Does it help take the story in the direction you want it to? Will it improve the reader's experience?

What if my editor wants me to change everything?

Perhaps they are not the right editor for you.

The editor should not fundamentally change your story or alter your creative vision. Their job is to help you shape your manuscript into a better version of itself, and retain your voice and ideas while at the same time improving it for the reader. This is a skillful balancing act, which is why experienced editors are so highly sought after.

How long will the editing process take?

This will depend on the type of writer you are in terms of the first draft. If you outline in great detail and spend time up front making the first draft the best it can be, then editing might take less time than for a discovery writer who only figures out the book after the first draft.

The more books you've written, the more you understand how to shape a novel, the more you can write a clean draft, so editing speeds up. That doesn't mean it gets easier to write a book, but it does mean you know how to find and fix issues.

It will also depend on the length of the book. A 50,000-word romance with one protagonist will be a faster edit than a 150,000-word sprawling fantasy with multiple point-of-view characters.

It will also depend on your experience, so don't compare your editing time to someone who has written a lot of books.

Give editing the time it needs. You want your book to be the best it can be. But also remember Parkinson's Law, which I discussed in chapter 4.7 on writing the first draft: "Work expands so as to fill the time available for its completion." This law also applies to editing.

Set your deadline and schedule your editing time accordingly. Don't book a professional editor until you've been through at least your self-editing process, as it may take longer than you think.

How much does an editor cost?

This will depend on the type of edit, your genre and word count, how experienced you are as a writer, and how much experience the editor has.

Editors usually quote a range on their website and you can also email and ask for a more detailed quote based on your manuscript length and sample.

Every dollar I have spent on editing has been worth it as an investment in my writing craft and the quality of my finished novels. Although my requirements are different now, I continue to use editors and proofreaders for all my books. The more eyes on your novel before publication, the better it will be on launch.

What if you have a tight budget?

When I started out as a writer, I had a day job and I saved up for the editorial process. It was an investment in my craft and a possible future creative career.

If you already have or intend to set up a business as a writer, then you can offset the cost of editors against any profits. But when you're starting out, you can't necessarily see that far ahead.

If you're on a tight budget, then find or set up a writer's group with others in your genre and work through one another's manuscripts. You might also have other skills you can barter for editing services, but remember that bartering is subject to tax in many jurisdictions, so don't assume that it is 'free.'

What if my editor steals my ideas or my manuscript?

This is a common concern of new writers who think that editors might run away with their book and make millions with their idea.

But don't worry, editors are professionals. They work within a contractual framework that protects both parties. So make sure you are happy with the contract before you sign it.

If you are really worried, you can register your copyright before you send the manuscript to anyone else. While it is not legally necessary to register copyright — it exists the moment the work is created — there are registration companies in every country that can provide peace of mind. Just search for 'copyright registration' within your territory.

Will I need different editors when I'm further along in my writing journey?

Yes, as your craft and experience improves, you will likely work with different editors. You might also choose to use a new editor for a different genre, or work with recommended professionals to take your craft to the next level.

Questions:

- How will you find a professional editor and validate that they are the right one for you?

- How will you work with your editor so you are both happy with the process and the result?

- How can you prepare yourself mentally for receiving feedback and line edits? How can you reframe the experience as positive and learn for next time?

Resources:

- My list of recommended editors: www.TheCreativePenn.com/editors

- Alliance of Independent Authors — www.TheCreativePenn.com/alliance

- The following editing associations offer directories and job posting services: The Editorial Freelancers Association (US), the Chartered Institute for Editing and Proofreading (UK), the Institute for Professional Editors (Australia and New Zealand), and Editors Canada.

5.4 Beta readers, specialist readers, and sensitivity readers

Professional editors approach your manuscript with a critical eye based on their knowledge of language, story structure, and genre. But sometimes, it's a good idea to gain perspective from readers who are not experts on sentence structure or grammar, but comment on the story itself, and their experience of reading it as a whole.

Beta readers

Beta readers are a trusted group of people who evaluate your book from a reader's perspective before publication. The term comes from the software industry, where early versions are tested in beta before being released to the public.

While there are some paid beta reader services, many authors find people from their existing readership, or from among genre fans in the writing community. Authors usually thank their beta readers in their acknowledgments.

Specialist readers

Specialist readers are experts on a particular topic who read with their expertise in mind. This might be a police officer who checks a crime novel, or a physicist who reads for a science-fiction author.

Sensitivity readers

Sensitivity readers check for cultural and diversity issues, lack of or clichéd representation, and insensitive, inauthentic, or uninformed language, characters, or situations.

This type of feedback can help an author before publication, and can be particularly useful if you are tackling more controversial topics. It can also be valuable when reviewing older manuscripts if you want to republish a new edition, as gendered language has changed, as well as the need for representation, diversity, and inclusivity.

While some criticize sensitivity reading as a step toward censorship, most authors want to make their books the best they can be, and ensure the reader experience is excellent, whatever the genre. Being a fiction writer is also about empathy — with our characters and with our readers — so improving our ability to write about diverse characters is important.

However, authors cannot be experts on what it's like to experience every race or religion, every body type or disability or mental health issue, or understand every country or culture. Feedback from different kinds of readers can help us write better stories, and it is the author's choice whether to implement suggestions in the final manuscript.

Do you need all of these types of readers?

No. You don't need any of them, or you can choose to use some of them for different books, depending on the need.

It's up to you (and your agent or publisher if you choose to go that route).

At what stage in the editorial process should you use these types of readers?

The book should be as close to the final version as possible. These people are reading with fresh eyes; if they read again later, they can never approach the story with such an open mind.

Most authors will send the manuscript to a select

group of readers after the main editorial revisions, but before the proofread. Some authors with more developed careers even use their team of beta readers instead of editors at different stages of the process.

What should you provide to readers?

Provide the manuscript in the format the reader prefers. This could be an MS Word document or PDF. Many established authors use Bookfunnel, which allows you to create a version that can be read on any reading device or phone.

Specialist readers and sensitivity readers have their specific expertise, but for more general beta readers, you need to provide some direction as to what you expect. For example:

- Did you skip over anything? Did anything bore you?
- Was anything confusing? Did you have to reread any parts?
- What did you like?
- Was there anything you hated or objected to or had a problem with?

How long should you give them to read?

Allow at least two weeks for readers to assess and provide feedback. Be clear on the timeline when you send them the book.

Do you need to make all the changes they suggest?

No, and if you try to, you will end up straying from your creative goal, messing up your author voice, and likely pleasing no one!

Keep your number of early readers small and specific to what you want to achieve. Assess each comment and suggestion on its own merit and decide whether or not to make the change.

Be confident in your creative vision and beware writing by committee, which becomes a problem if you ask too many people for feedback. Only you can decide what you want for your novel.

Questions:

- What kind of readers might be useful for your manuscript?
- Where will you find these readers?
- How do you hope to improve the manuscript from this feedback?
- How will you assess whether to make the changes?

Resources:

- The Reedsy marketplace includes different kinds of editors, beta readers, and sensitivity readers — www.TheCreativePenn.com/reedsy
- Directory of sensitivity readers — www.writingdiversely.com/directory
- Editors of Color — editorsofcolor.com

5.5 Editing tools and software

While there are no rules for creativity, there are certainly rules for writing coherently.

If you read *The Elements of Style* by Strunk and White, you will grasp the basics of grammar and effective writing, but there are also tools that can help us with the technicalities. The most popular are ProWritingAid, Grammarly, and Hemingway. It's worth trying them to find which you prefer.

Why I use and recommend ProWritingAid

I've tried several tools and now use and recommend ProWritingAid as the best option for fiction. It integrates with all kinds of word-processing options so you can use it with whatever software you use to write, but it is the only one that integrates with Scrivener (at the time of writing).

When I've finished my first draft, I open ProWritingAid and then open my Scrivener project within it. I work through each chapter and make appropriate changes. Then I print out the first draft.

After each draft, I do the same thing, essentially using the tool to improve my manuscript as much as possible before I send it to my human editor.

You can find ProWritingAid at:

www.TheCreativePenn.com/prowritingaid

For more detail, check out my tutorial:

www.TheCreativePenn.com/prowritingaidtutorial

Do you need to make every change the editing software suggests?

Definitely not.

Review each change and consider whether or not it helps the story, or whether it's appropriate. I follow about 80 percent of the suggestions.

Do I still need a human editor if I use editing software?

Yes. While software can help with many aspects, it cannot read your manuscript as a whole and pick up issues that may jar readers, or discover inconsistencies in the story.

I use ProWritingAid before I send to my editor,

and also before publication for one final check. It is incredibly valuable, but it doesn't replace an editor's view of the whole manuscript.

"Using software is cheating. You're not a real writer unless you learn and apply all the grammar and writing rules yourself."

You don't have to use editing software. You're welcome to learn all the rules and apply them. It's up to you.

But consider whether you use tools in other areas of your writing life.

Do you use a computer to write instead of writing by hand? Do you use Google to search instead of looking up everything in a library of printed books? Do you use apps on your phone for anything useful?

Humans use tools to improve all areas of life, so why not use a tool to help improve your writing, learn the craft, and enable your editor to focus on the things that humans are best at?

Questions:

- How could you use software to improve your editing process?

Resources:

- *Dreyer's English: An Utterly Correct Guide to Clarity and Style* — Benjamin Dreyer
- *Eats, Shoots and Leaves: The Zero Tolerance Approach to Punctuation* — Lynne Truss
- *The Elements of Style* — William Strunk Jr. and E.B. White
- *The Language of Fiction: A Writer's Stylebook* — Brian Shawver
- ProWritingAid software — www.TheCreativePenn.com/prowritingaid
- Tutorial on using ProWritingAid for your novel — www.TheCreativePenn.com/prowritingaidtutorial
- Grammarly — www.TheCreativePenn.com/grammarly
- Hemingway — www.hemingwayapp.com

5.6 Lessons learned from editing my first novel after more than a decade

In the first quarter of 2022, I re-edited my first three novels, *Stone of Fire*, *Crypt of Bone*, and *Ark of Blood*, written over a decade ago from 2009 to 2012.

The process of rewriting was the catalyst for me to finally finish this book after many years of resistance. Although there is always more to learn, the experience solidified my knowledge of the craft.

I shared a version of this chapter as a podcast episode, and many authors found my experience useful and reassuring. Others questioned my decision, so I've included this edited version to outline the process and also my lessons learned as they may help with your edits, regardless of where you are in the author journey.

Surely when a book is published, it's done — you can never go back

Writers and publishers have always re-issued books in new editions, with rewrites, corrections, updates, and other changes.

If you publish independently, it is a simple matter of uploading new files, but if you publish traditionally, you will need to go through your publisher. Most of these changes are minor, fixing typos or issues that have emerged over time, but they can also be more substantial.

In March 2022, Booker Prize–winning author Ben Okri announced a new version of his 2008 novel *Starbook* in the *Guardian*. He spent five years rewriting it "to give more emphasis to transatlantic slavery," and retitled it as *The Last Gift of the Master Artists*.

The article noted other fiction authors who rewrote their novels, including Charles Dickens, who heavily edited *Oliver Twist* in a later edition after a complaint from a Jewish woman about antisemitism.

Okri acknowledged, "There is perhaps nothing to gain for me from this but a good artistic night's sleep." But if a book nudges at you for long enough, eventually, you have to listen.

Why I decided to rewrite when so much advice says 'never go back'

There was nothing particularly wrong with my first three novels. Between them, they had several thousand reviews across the various online stores with over a four-star average.

But I knew I could improve them.

Stone of Fire was my first novel, but it's also the first in my ARKANE action-adventure thriller series of a dozen books.

It's my permanently free first-in-series ebook, the one I repeatedly advertise to bring new readers into my writing. So, it's important for my fiction marketing efforts and, as the first in series, it's the primary way readers enter my ARKANE world.

Morgan Sierra, my protagonist, is also my alter ego. Sure, she's an ex-Israeli military psychologist, Oxford University professor, and Krav Maga expert — but her thoughts are often my own, or at least represent some facet of my personality.

Like me, Morgan is fascinated with religion and

travels the world. I visit interesting locations for research, while she investigates supernatural mysteries alongside Jake Timber and the rest of the ARKANE team.

The advice from many writing coaches and experts is to leave your old series behind, and write a new one. In this way, you can improve your craft and reach readers without rewriting old books.

But I can't leave Morgan behind. And neither can my hardcore readers, who love the ARKANE series and demand a new one as soon as I deliver the latest story.

I've written other series — my Mapwalker fantasy trilogy and my Brooke and Daniel crime thrillers — and various stand-alone stories. But in terms of action-adventure, I'm invested in Morgan and the ARKANE team.

The ARKANE thrillers appeal to fans of other long-running series like James Rollins's Sigma series, Steve Berry's Cotton Malone series, Lincoln and Child's Pendergast series, and thrillers by Greig Beck, J. Robert Kennedy, and R.D. Brady. They are action-adventure conspiracy thrillers with aspects of the supernatural.

I love this kind of long-running thriller series and always set out to write books for the 'old me' who read on the commuter train on the way to a job I hated.

But the Jo who wrote those first three novels in 2009 to 2012 had a lot to learn. She tried her best, and she worked with professional editors — but I am not that writer anymore.

My craft has improved over many years and many books published, as well as through classes, books, and reading thousands more thrillers for pleasure. I've also worked with various different professional editors and proofreaders, and now augment my craft with tools like ProWritingAid, which didn't exist when I started out.

I didn't want to "just start another series" in order to demonstrate improvement in my craft, so I rewrote the first three books to bring them up to my current standard.

How *Stone of Fire* developed from 2009 to 2022

In order to look forward, it's important to look back.

I started the story during NaNoWriMo, National Novel Writing Month, in 2009. I knew I needed more help, so I joined The Year of the Novel at Queensland Library in Brisbane, Australia, where I lived back then.

After finishing the first draft in 2010, I worked with several professional editors and then independently published *Pentecost* (as it was originally called) in April 2011. I documented the entire process with blog posts and videos, so if you want to step back in time and have a laugh at a younger me, check them out at www.TheCreativePenn.com/firstnovel

I wrote two more ARKANE novels, *Prophecy* and *Exodus*, in the subsequent years, and my early reviews proved a couple of things.

Readers enjoyed the books, and they have always had good reviews. But the cover branding and book titles positioned them more as Christian fiction. The stories feature historical and biblical locations, artifacts, and questions of faith, but I am not a Christian and it was never my intention to position the stories that way.

The ARKANE thrillers are more like Dan Brown's *The Da Vinci Code*. They skirt the edge of religious myth and history, but are essentially global action-adventure thrillers with deeper questions at their heart.

I needed to figure out how to reposition them.

Many authors grapple with this question of genre and market fit, and I struggled just as much as anyone. I go into more detail in *How to Market a Book*, if you are interested in the more commercial side of the author life.

During those early years, I met with a few agents who were interested in working together, one in the USA and one in the UK. Ultimately, they didn't work out, but they helped me with repositioning and we parted on good terms. (Note: It is not uncommon for authors and agents to part ways. It's a business relationship, and it has to serve both parties to be successful.)

In 2015, I rebranded the first three books as *Stone of Fire*, *Crypt of Bone*, and *Ark of Blood*. I commissioned new covers and also did a light edit of *Stone of Fire* to add more emotional beats than the original version.

Over the years since, I've updated back matter and fixed typos, but there hasn't been a substantial re-edit.

My re-writing process

I started with the existing version as a new first draft. As I format my ebooks using Vellum, I exported the ebook from Vellum as a rich text format (RTF) file and saved as an MS Word document.

If you go through this process, you might have the master file in other formats, but make sure you re-edit the correct version.

I imported this MS Word document into a new Scrivener project, which became my new first draft.

I used ProWritingAid in a first pass edit to fix certain issues, as detailed in the craft section below, and improved the overall chapter score from 65 percent to over 90 percent, an invaluable first step.

Every day I worked on the manuscript, I exported and backed it up as detailed in chapter 4.6.

Once all the chapters were finished, I exported from Scrivener back to MS Word and printed out the full draft.

I followed my usual editing process: editing by hand on paper, then updating the master Scrivener project, printing and editing again, then running it through ProWritingAid, exporting to MS Word, and submitting to my editor.

When the edits came back, I went through the MS Word document with Track Changes, accepted or rejected them and fixed issues, then the manuscript had a proofreading check before re-publication.

Craft notes on rewriting after more than a decade

There is an anecdotal saying amongst writers that after a million words published, you know what you're doing. Or at least, you have a better idea of what to improve next!

I've published several million words now, most of those since I wrote *Stone of Fire*, and I've also spent time improving my craft through training and deliberate practice.

Here are some improvements I made in the rewrite which might help you, whether you're editing your first or twenty-first novel.

Increased depth of character, emotion, and character point of view

Depth of character is all about point of view (POV). Although I understood each chapter needed a POV in the beginning, I had not sunk deep enough into each person.

For example, "Morgan saw that the door was open," became "The door was open." I am in Morgan's POV, so I can write from her frame of reference. To take another example: "Morgan thought that perhaps Jake might need help," becomes "Jake needed help."

The use of '[character name] thought' or including thoughts in italics isn't usually necessary because the chapter should be in the POV of the characters. However, this is a stylistic choice and many authors use it.

I also increased depth and emotion by including more detail about the character's response to a situation and their internal feelings, rather than just their external actions.

We read fiction to gain insight into someone else's life, to experience vicariously, and understanding the character's point of view is part of the joy of reading. In my early drafts, Morgan reacted with external action and physical movement, but the reader didn't necessarily know why. This time around, I could write more emotionally because, after a dozen ARKANE thrillers, I know my characters so well.

My recurring series characters, Morgan and Jake, and others like Father Ben and Martin, are more real to me now. I found myself saying, 'Morgan wouldn't do that' or 'Jake wouldn't say that' as I went through the process. I couldn't have known those things a decade ago because I hadn't written all the other books and I'm a discovery writer.

Leaned into my author voice

When I started writing, I was afraid to let people see what was inside my mind. I've always struggled with fear of judgment, and I'm a people-pleaser at heart. I want people to like me, to think I'm useful and a 'good girl' and an upstanding member of the community.

But, actually, that's Joanna Penn, the nonfiction, self-help side of me you're reading right now.

My fiction self, J.F. Penn, is darker, an old soul, with deeper currents under the surface. I needed time to discover that side of me and the confidence to stop self-censoring, to write what I truly wanted to.

J.F. Penn is my rebellious side, my inner Goth, who loves crypts and ossuaries, as well as cathedrals and galleries. She writes about good and evil, right and wrong, angels and demons — and she loves a fast-paced book (or movie) with a high body count and plenty of explosions.

At points in this re-edit of *Stone of Fire*, I glimpsed my future author voice, but I sensed my early writer self backing away for fear of being judged.

But now I embrace my voice, and in the rewrite, I doubled down on the intensity.

Improved pacing

The first edition of *Stone of Fire* was written more like a literary novel, with long, complicated sentences, overly long paragraphs, and slower pacing than a typical thriller. After reading many thousands of thrillers in the last decade, and studying pace in particular, I made a few specific changes.

I used more line breaks, more paragraph breaks, shorter sentences where appropriate, sentence fragments, and faster dialogue. These increase white space on a page, which means it's faster for the reader's eye to scan, and they have to turn the page to get to the rest of the story.

This time around, I split scenes across the end of chapters so the reader would have to start a new one to find out more.

I changed the order of some scenes to vary pacing, so there were slower-paced chapters in between the action to give the reader a respite.

I overused dates and timestamps in the early editions, as well as other overly obvious timeline details, but I found I could remove those without affecting the story, which made it smoother for the reader.

They were important for me as a writer to make sure each character was where they needed to be at the right time, but they weren't needed in the final text. I could show morning by early sunlight or the passing of time with a mention of 'next day,' or other phrases instead of time stamps.

Reduced info-dumps

I love, love, love my research!

One of the main reasons I write fiction is so I can go deep into the research process and spin real-world events, places, artifacts, and people into story. But including too much research in the text can slow pacing and may cause the reader to skip parts of the story.

Equally, one of my hallmarks as J.F. Penn is sparking curiosity in the reader. Many of my readers email to say they google things to find out what's true and they love my Author's Note at the back of the books, in which I discuss my inspirations and research for each novel. So it's a fine line in terms of what to leave in, what to edit down, and what to remove completely.

In some cases, I had repeated the same information several times by telling different characters the same thing. But not every character needed to know all that information, and it was *the reader* I really needed to think about.

Changed verbs to make them more active (where appropriate)

Passive writing is a common issue for new writers, and especially those of us who come from the world of legal or business writing, where hedging your bets rather than making strong statements is more common.

You can often spot passive writing by noting whether the word 'was' is necessary.

"The statue of St James was surrounded by pilgrims" becomes "Pilgrims surrounded the statue of St. James."

In another example, "Morgan was running" becomes "Morgan ran."

Of course, you don't want to change everything.

Just be aware of your options. As ever, it's a fine line that you learn with experience, and writing tools like ProWritingAid can help immensely. I wish I'd had it when I started out!

Resolved dialogue issues and improved for audio

I wrote *Stone of Fire* before the rise of audiobooks so I overused 'said,' and needed to fix many of the issues covered in chapter 3.5 in terms of too many names, on-the-nose dialogue, repeated sounds, and more.

Rephrased 'started to' and 'began to'

I rephrased lots of these standard phrases. Sometimes they are necessary, but I overused them.

For example, I changed "He began to pray" to "He prayed."

"She started to walk" to "She walked."

"She said with a whisper" to "She whispered."

I also checked my use of adverbs like 'actually,' 'really,' 'very,' and 'suddenly,' and changed obvious clichés to something more original.

Rephrased disembodied body part action

This is a surprisingly common issue and, once you're aware of it, you will see it everywhere!

For example, "Her hands held him down" becomes "She held him down."

"Morgan's eyebrows raised in surprise" becomes "Morgan raised an eyebrow."

"Her mouth whispered a prayer" becomes "She whispered a prayer."

"His eyes were fixed on the screen" becomes "He gazed at the screen."

Rephrased for inclusivity and checked diversity

I'm English, so I have a keen sense of hierarchy. It is part of our national identity, and if you watch *The Crown* on Netflix, you'll understand why.

When I wrote *Stone of Fire* back in 2009 to 2011, I worked in a hierarchical office world and I found phrasing in this edit that I wouldn't use now, and that has changed in the cultural shifts of more than a decade.

For example, one character addressed another as 'sir' when they were not in the military, which read as completely out of place this time around.

I changed some gendered language to gender-neutral, where appropriate. 'Mankind' became 'humanity.' 'Policeman' became 'police officer.'

ProWritingAid has an inclusive language filter that helps identify phrasing that might need revisiting, although, of course, it is up to you to fix what you think is appropriate.

Updated technology

Technology inevitably moves on, and it was quite funny to read some of my old phrasing.

I changed 'smart phone' to 'phone' and 'mini-copter' to 'drone,' and removed some dates which were in the future when I wrote the book, but are now meaningless.

I also updated my description of the prototype virtual reality (VR) library the ARKANE investigators use in their research to make it reflect a world where VR is more common.

Reduced word count

These changes reduced the word count in *Stone of Fire* from around 72,000 to nearer 55,000, which is the usual length for my ARKANE thrillers. The other two books had less of a dramatic change, as my craft improved even over the first three books.

Back when I started out, when the digital revolution was in its early days, I was told that a book had to be over 70,000 words to be published, so I padded the manuscript out with extra scenes that I removed in this edit.

Don't readers complain about new editions?

Importantly, I did not change the story.

The plot and characters are the same, and if you read my first three novels in the previous editions, you don't need to re-read them. The changes are more for readability and style, pacing, character depth, and author voice.

New readers won't notice as they will read the latest version. If you republish, make sure to update the copyright page to the new edition, and if it's a new title, include the phrase "previously published as…" on your sales description and within the book.

Was it worth rewriting?

It took three and a half months of my time, as well as the costs of re-editing and republishing, but it was well worth it for me.

As with Ben Okri, it gives me "a good artistic night's sleep" to know that the books represent my current writing style, and that readers can enter my ARKANE world in the best way possible.

The process also solidified my thoughts on the writing craft and gave me the confidence to write this book, as it helped me see how far I've come.

Only you can decide whether such a rewrite is useful for your situation. It's certainly not for everyone. If you are considering it, then make sure enough time has passed before you rewrite.

Questions:

- Why are you considering a rewrite? What benefits do you expect to gain from the process? What will make it worth it for you?

- How long has it been since the original release? Is this long enough to make a rewrite worthwhile?

- If you're editing for the first time, what aspects might you need to look out for in your manuscript?

Resources:

- "Booker winner Ben Okri rewrites published novel to drive home message on slavery," *The Guardian*, 19 March 2022 — www.theguardian.com/books/2022/mar/19/booker-winner-ben-okri-rewrites-published-novel-to-drive-home-message-on-slavery

- Blog posts and videos about my first novel process
  — www.TheCreativePenn.com/firstnovel

- "Writing tips: Lessons learned from rewriting my first novel over a decade later" The Creative Penn Podcast, Feb 25, 2022 — www.TheCreativePenn.com/2022/02/25/writing-tips-rewriting-my-first-novel

- ProWritingAid
  — www.TheCreativePenn.com/prowritingaid

- ProWritingAid tutorial — www.TheCreativePenn.com/prowritingaidtutorial

- Vellum — www.TheCreativePenn.com/vellum

- Vellum tutorial — www.TheCreativePenn.com/vellum-tutorial

5.7 When is the book finished?

> "I have not yet found words to truly convey the intensity of this remembered rapture—that moment of exquisite joy when necessary words come together and the work is complete, finished, ready to be read."
>
> —bell hooks, *Remembered Rapture*

You can edit a book forever if you want to.

Every time you read it, you will find things to change. Every time you hire another editor, they will find more. If you work with beta readers, they will also offer opinions.

Your novel will never be finished — until you decide it is.

Nothing is ever perfect. Even if you hire three separate editors and use multiple proofreaders, you will still find a typo or an error in the published novel. Pick up any bestselling book from a traditional publisher, and you will still find an issue somewhere. It happens to everyone.

Look at any prize-winning or bestselling book on Amazon and check the reviews. The more popular the book, the more issues people will find with it. There will never be a novel that satisfies everyone, and that's fine.

Of course, you must make sure your book is the best it can be, but set boundaries for yourself so you do eventually finish.

- Have you self-edited your manuscript?
- Have you worked with a professional editor, or at least worked through the manuscript with other writers to improve it?
- Have you used editing tools and/or a proofreader?
- Have you set a deadline to move into the publishing process so you are not editing forever?

If you have been through this rigorous editorial process and you still feel the itch to edit again, be honest with yourself.

Is another round of changes really going to make a substantial difference to this book?

Would it be better to work on the next novel instead of constantly reworking this one?

Are you struggling with fear of judgment, fear of failure, procrastination, or other mindset issues that you need to work on instead of editing? Check out my book *The Successful Author Mindset* if you think this might be the case.

Strive for excellence, do your best, and then release your book out into the world.

"Set a limit on revisions, set a limit on drafts, set a time limit… The book will never be perfect."

—*Kristine Kathryn Rusch, The Pursuit of Perfection and How it Harms Writers*

Questions:

- Have you followed an editorial process to make your book the best it can be within a specific time limit?
- If you're still struggling with the pursuit of perfection, what can you do to move past that?

Resources:

- *The Pursuit of Perfection: And How it Harms Writers* — Kristine Kathryn Rusch
- *The Successful Author Mindset: A Handbook for Surviving the Writer's Journey* — Joanna Penn
- *Remembered Rapture: The Writer at Work* — bell hooks

Conclusion

Writing is simple, but no one said it was easy.

If you're feeling overwhelmed, remember the metaphor of the iceberg.

There are only a few things you need to get started, and you can learn all the hidden depths of the craft over the rest of your writing career.

What do you need to do right now to take the next step?

Go back to basics of story

Keep it simple. All you need is:

- A character
- In a setting
- Who has a goal
- And who has to overcome conflict on the way to achieving that goal while

- Someone or something tries to stop them.
- They either achieve their goal or fail
- And along the way, they go through some kind of transformation

If you're lost in your novel, take a step back and distill it down to these things.

Go back to the basics of writing

Open a blank page in your notebook or on whatever device you write on.

Set a timer for five minutes.

Write.

Stay motivated

When I started writing fiction, I didn't know any authors or even anyone who wrote. I worked my day job as an IT consultant, and I couldn't talk about my creative dreams. It was lonely as I had no community.

I started listening to podcasts and audiobooks and I followed writers on Twitter, which was new back then. I read motivational self-help books and kept myself going with affirmations that I slowly turned into reality.

I still do these things, because we all need motivation to make it through the difficult times.

I have a cork board by my desk with quotes pinned on it. Here are a couple of them:

"Have you made art today? Have you written 1000 words? Are you a step closer?"

"Measure your life by what you create."

"Trust emergence."

"Huge shifts in ambition require huge shifts in behavior."

You need to find ways of motivating yourself. Whatever works to keep yourself going.

I share more tips in *The Successful Author Mindset*, and you can join me every Monday on The Creative Penn Podcast, available on your preferred podcast app. I always share personal updates about my writing — including the difficulties! — as well as interviews and resources.

Don't get distracted by publishing and book marketing

There is a lot of information out there on publishing and book marketing, and a great deal of advice about the best way to reach readers, sell more books, and make money as a writer. I have other books that cover those topics if you want to learn more.

But if you have not finished a first draft and self-edited your novel yet, ignore it all.

It is a distraction.

You have nothing to publish and nothing to market if you have no book.

Get back to writing and think about the rest of it later.

Write the next book

"When I ask you to write more books, I am urging you to do what will be for your own good and for the good of the world at large."

—Virginia Woolf, *A Room of One's Own*

Writers write.

We can't help ourselves.

It's how we discover what we think. It's how we express ourselves. It's how we help other people. It's how we live.

Writing my first novel changed my life, although perhaps not in the way that I hoped!

I did not hit the bestseller lists and make millions. In fact, barely anyone even noticed when my first novel came out into the world.

But it freed my imagination, and I stepped into a new way of life. I held my first finished novel in my hand and I knew I could make it as a writer.

I had so many ideas for stories once I'd written that first one. The experience of writing opened the floodgates of creativity. I got the bug! Perhaps you will, too.

I wish you all the best with your novel. May it change your life.

Happy writing!

* * *

You can download the questions, bibliography, and more resources at:

www.TheCreativePenn.com/writenoveldownload

If you'd like to work through the material in writing, you can find the print edition of *How to Write a Novel: Companion Workbook* at:

www.TheCreativePenn.com/writenovelworkbook

"Writing a novel will change your life."

—Joanna Penn

Need more help?

Sign up for my *free* Author Blueprint and email series, and receive useful information on writing, publishing, book marketing, and making a living with your writing:

www.TheCreativePenn.com/blueprint

* * *

Love podcasts?

Join me every Monday for The Creative Penn Podcast where I talk about writing, publishing, book marketing and the author business.

Available on your favorite podcast app.

Find the backlist episodes at:

www.TheCreativePenn.com/podcast

More Books And Courses From Joanna Penn

Non-Fiction Books for Authors

How to Write Non-Fiction

How to Market a Book

How to Make a Living with your Writing

Productivity for Authors

Successful Self-Publishing

Your Author Business Plan

The Successful Author Mindset

The Relaxed Author

Public Speaking for Authors, Creatives and Other Introverts

Audio for Authors: Audiobooks, Podcasting, and Voice Technologies

The Healthy Writer

Business for Authors

Co-writing a Book

Career Change

Artificial Intelligence, Blockchain, and Virtual Worlds

www.TheCreativePenn.com/books

Courses for Authors

How to Write a Novel

How to Write Non-Fiction

Multiple Streams of Income from your Writing

Your Author Business Plan

Content Marketing for Fiction

Productivity for Authors

Turn What You Know Into An Online Course

The AI-Assisted Author

Co-Writing a Book

www.TheCreativePenn.com/courses

Fiction as J.F. Penn

ARKANE Action-adventure Thrillers

Stone of Fire #1
Crypt of Bone #2
Ark of Blood #3
One Day in Budapest #4
Day of the Vikings #5
Gates of Hell #6
One Day in New York #7
Destroyer of Worlds #8
End of Days #9

Valley of Dry Bones #10
Tree of Life #11
Tomb of Relics #12

Brooke and Daniel Crime Thrillers

Desecration #1
Delirium #2
Deviance #3

Mapwalker Dark Fantasy Trilogy

Map of Shadows #1
Map of Plagues #2
Map of the Impossible #3

Other Books and Short Stories

Risen Gods

A Thousand Fiendish Angels:
Short stories based on Dante's Inferno

The Dark Queen: An Underwater Archaeology Short Story

Blood, Sweat, and Flame

A Midwinter Sacrifice

More books coming soon.

You can sign up to be notified of new releases, giveaways and pre-release specials - plus, get a free book!

www.JFPenn.com/free

About Joanna Penn

Joanna Penn writes non-fiction for authors and is an award-nominated, New York Times and USA Today bestselling thriller author as J.F. Penn.

She's also an award-winning podcaster, creative entrepreneur, and international professional speaker. She lives in Bath, England with her husband and enjoys a nice G&T.

Joanna's award-winning site for writers, TheCreativePenn.com, helps people to write, publish and market their books through articles, audio, video and online products as well as live workshops.

Get your free Author Blueprint:
www.TheCreativePenn.com/blueprint

Love thrillers? www.JFPenn.com

Love travel? Check out my Books and Travel podcast: www.BooksAndTravel.page

Connect with Joanna

www.TheCreativePenn.com
joanna@TheCreativePenn.com

www.twitter.com/thecreativepenn
www.facebook.com/TheCreativePenn
www.Instagram.com/jfpennauthor
www.youtube.com/thecreativepenn

Appendix 1: Bibliography

You can download the questions, bibliography, and more resources at www.TheCreativePenn.com/writenoveldownload

30 Days of Worldbuilding: An Author's Step-by-Step Guide to Building Fictional Worlds — A. Trevena

2,000 to 10,000: Writing Faster, Writing Better, and Writing More of What You Love — Rachel Aaron

5,000 Words Per Hour: Write Faster, Write Smarter — Chris Fox

A Beautiful Anarchy: When The Life Creative Becomes The Life Created — David duChemin

Anatomy of Story: 22 Steps to Becoming a Master Storyteller — John Truby

Audio for Authors: Audiobooks, Podcasting and Voice Technologies — Joanna Penn

Big Magic: Creative Living Beyond Fear — Elizabeth Gilbert

Bird by Bird: Some Instructions on Writing and Life — Anne Lamott

Books Are Made Out of Books: A Guide to Cormac McCarthy's Literary Influences — Michael Lynn Crews

Conquering Writer's Block and Summoning Inspiration: Learn to Nurture a Lifestyle of Creativity — K.M. Weiland

Create a World Clinic — Holly Lisle

Creating Character Arcs: The Masterful Author's Guide to Uniting Story Structure, Plot, and Character Development — K.M. Weiland

Dear Writer, Are You Intuitive? — Becca Syme and Susan Bischoff

Dialogue: The Art of Verbal Action for Page, Stage, and Screen — Robert McKee

Dictate your Book: How to Write Your Book Faster, Better, and Smarter — Monica Leonelle

Dreyer's English: An Utterly Correct Guide to Clarity and Style — Benjamin Dreyer

Eats, Shoots and Leaves: The Zero Tolerance Approach to Punctuation — Lynne Truss

Evil Plans: Having Fun on the Road to World Domination — Hugh MacLeod

Fantasy Mapping: Drawing Worlds — Wesley Jones

Foolproof Dictation: A No-Nonsense System for Effective & Rewarding Dictation — Christopher Downing

Free Within Ourselves: Fiction Lessons for Black Authors — Jewell Parker Rhodes

Find Your Artistic Voice: The Essential Guide to Working Your Creative Magic — Lisa Congdon

GMC: Goal, Motivation, Conflict: The Building Blocks of Good Fiction — Debra Dixon

Heinlein's Rules: Five Simple Business Rules for Writing — Dean Wesley Smith

How to Write a Series: A Guide to Series Types and Structure plus Troubleshooting Tips and Marketing Tactics — Sara Rosett

How to Write Dazzling Dialogue: The Fastest Way to Improve Any Manuscript — James Scott Bell

If You Want to Write — Brenda Ueland

Intuitive Editing: A Creative and Practical Guide to Revising Your Manuscript — Tiffany Yates Martin

Make Good Art — Neil Gaiman

Mastering Plot Twists: How to Use Suspense, Targeted Storytelling Strategies, and Structure to Captivate Your Readers — Jane K. Cleland

Mental Fight — Ben Okri

Nail Your Novel: Writing Characters Who'll Keep Readers Captivated — Roz Morris

On Being A Dictator: Using Dictation To Be a Better Writer — Kevin J. Anderson and Martin L. Shoemaker

On Writing: A Memoir of the Craft — Stephen King

Outlining Your Novel: Map Your Way to Success — K.M. Weiland

Plot and Structure: Techniques and Exercises for Crafting a Plot that Grips Readers from Start to Finish — James Scott Bell

Point of View: How to use the different POV types, avoid head-hopping, and choose the best point of view for your book — Sandra Gerth

Productivity for Authors: Find Time to Write, Organize Your Author Life, and Decide What Really Matters — Joanna Penn

Remembered Rapture: The Writer at Work — bell hooks

Research Like A Librarian: Research Help and Tips for Writers for Researching in the Digital Age — Vikki J. Carter, The Author's Librarian

Romance Your Brand: Building a Marketable Genre Fiction Series — Zoe York

Romancing the Beat: Story Structure for Romance Novels — Gwen Hayes

Save the Cat! Writes a Novel: The Last Book on Novel Writing You'll Ever Need — Jessica Brody

Self-Editing for Fiction Writers: How to Edit Yourself into Print — Renni Browne and Dave King

Song of Myself — Walt Whitman

Song of Solomon — Toni Morrison

Steal Like An Artist: 10 Things Nobody Told You About Being Creative — Austin Kleon

Steering The Craft: A Twenty-First Century Guide to Sailing the Sea of Story — Ursula K. Le Guin

Story Genius: How to Use Brain Science to Go Beyond Outlining and Write a Riveting Novel — Lisa Cron

Story: Substance, Structure, Style, and The Principles of Screenwriting — Robert McKee

Story Engineering: Mastering the 6 Core Competencies of Successful Writing — Larry Brooks

Succulent Wild Woman: Dancing with Your Wonderfull Self — SARK

Take Off Your Pants! Outline Your Books for Faster, Better Writing — Libbie Hawker

The Artist's Way: A Spiritual Path to Higher Creativity — Julia Cameron

The Conflict Thesaurus: A Writer's Guide to Obstacles, Adversaries, and Inner Struggles — Angela Ackerman and Becca Puglisi

The Creative Habit: Learn It and Use It for Life — Twyla Tharp

The Elements of Style — William Strunk Jr. and E.B. White

The Emotion Thesaurus: A Writer's Guide to Character Expression — Angela Ackerman and Becca Puglisi

The Emotional Wound Thesaurus: A Writer's Guide to Psychological Trauma — Becca Puglisi and Angela Ackerman

The First Five Pages: A Writer's Guide to Staying Out of the Rejection Pile — Noah Lukeman

The Hero with a Thousand Faces — Joseph Campbell

The Heroine with 1001 Faces — Maria Tatar

The Heroine's Journey: For Writers, Readers, and Fans of Pop Culture — Gail Carriger

The Language of Fiction: A Writer's Stylebook — Brian Shawver

The Last Fifty Pages: The Art and Craft of Unforgettable Endings — James Scott Bell

The Last Lecture: Lessons in Living — Randy Pausch

The Novel Editing Workbook: 105 Tricks and Tips for Revising Your Manuscript — Kris Spisak

The Novel Writer's Toolkit: From Idea to Best-Seller — Bob Mayer

The Pursuit of Perfection: And How it Harms Writers — Kristine Kathryn Rusch

The Science of Storytelling: Why Stories Make Us Human, and How To Tell Them Better — Will Storr

The Stages of a Fiction Writer: Know Where You Stand on the Path to Writing — Dean Wesley Smith

The Story Grid: What Good Editors Know — Shawn Coyne

The Successful Author Mindset: A Handbook for Surviving the Writer's Journey — Joanna Penn

The Writer's Guide to Training your Dragon: Using Speech Recognition Software to Dictate Your Book and Supercharge Your Writing Workflow — Scott Baker

The Writer's Journey: Mythic Structure for Writers — Christopher Vogler

Three Story Method: Writing Scenes — J. Thorn

Voice: The Secret Power of Great Writing — James Scott Bell

Wired for Story: The Writer's Guide to Using Brain Science to Hook Readers from the Very First Sentence — Lisa Cron

Wonderbook: The Illustrated Guide to Creating Imaginative Fiction — Jeff VanderMeer

Writing Down the Bones: Freeing the Writer Within — Natalie Goldberg

Writing into the Dark: How to Write a Novel Without an Outline — Dean Wesley Smith

Writing the Novel From Plot to Print to Pixel — Lawrence Block

Writing the Other: A Practical Approach — Nisi Shawl and Cynthia Ward

Write to Market: Deliver a Book That Sells — Chris Fox

Writing Your Story's Theme: The Writer's Guide to Plotting Stories That Matter — K.M. Weiland

Your First Page: First Pages and What They Tell Us about the Pages that Follow Them — Peter Selgin

Appendix 2: List of Questions

You can download the questions, bibliography, and more resources at www.TheCreativePenn.com/writenoveldownload

If you'd like to work through the material in writing, you can find the print edition of *How to Write a Novel: Companion Workbook* at www.TheCreativePenn.com/writenovelworkbook

1.1 Why are you writing a novel?

- Why do you want to write a novel?
- Go deeper. What are the reasons behind that?
- Are these reasons enough to carry you through difficult times?

1.2 What has stopped you from completing a novel before?

- How long have you been thinking about writing a novel?

- Why haven't you written your novel before? Or, if you started, why didn't you finish? What stopped you — and how can you break through that barrier now?

- Are you going to finish the novel this time?

1.3 Principles to keep in mind as you create

- What do you already know about your personality and your lifestyle that might impact your writing craft?

- Have you tried different personality tests? If you haven't, how might they help you?

- How can you remain aware of what creative practices work for you along the way?

- What are the books (and films) that you truly love, rather than the ones you have been told to value by others? Write your list of five to ten.

- Do you already have a timed writing practice?

If not, do it now. Open a blank page. Find a writing prompt, or just start with "I remember..." Set a timer for ten minutes. Write.

- If you feel resistance to this practice, identify why and how you might overcome it.
- How can you keep your story simple?
- What is your writing age? What is the writing age of the author whose work you love the most?

2.1 How to find and capture ideas

- Are you brimming with story ideas already? Where do they come from? (If you aren't, don't worry!)
- How can you recognize your curiosity and lean into it?
- What could you do for an Artist's Date? Book one into your schedule soon.
- What fascinates you about people? How might those things turn into facets of character?
- What objects and artifacts interest you?
- What real events and places spark your curiosity?

- Consider the 'what if' questions behind the books you love, or other well-known books. How could you spin those in a new direction for your story?
- What quotes resonate with you?
- What themes and societal issues do you care about?
- What other books or myths or stories spark ideas for you?
- What aspects of your life could you mine for ideas?
- How will you capture your ideas?
- Are you worried about whether your ideas are unoriginal, or that someone will steal your ideas? If yes, how can you ease those fears?
- How will you choose which idea to work on?

2.2 How to research your novel and when to stop

- Do you enjoy research? How could you make research part of your writing process?
- What kinds of research will you do for your book?

- How can you avoid plagiarism?
- How will you know when to stop researching?

2.3 Outlining (or plotting)

- What are the benefits of outlining?
- What are the potential difficulties?
- Are you excited about the prospect of outlining? Or is it something you feel like you 'should' do?
- Which methods of outlining might work best for you?
- How much time do you want to spend outlining before you move on to writing?

2.4 Discovery writing (or pantsing)

- What are the benefits of discovery writing?
- What are the potential difficulties?
- Are you excited about the prospect of discovery writing? Does the empty page scare you or represent unlimited possibility?
- How do you think discovery writing might fit into your process?

2.5 What are you writing? Genre

- How can understanding genre help you as an author?

- Do you know what genre you're writing in? Don't worry if you don't, but perhaps you already have some idea.

- What makes a satisfying story for you? Think of your top five books, as well as your favorite movies and/or TV shows. Why are they so satisfying? What do you love about them?

- Choose five to ten books that are like what you're writing, which may be different from the books chosen above. Research their categories on Amazon. Are there commonalities? Might you be writing cross-genre?

- What genre conventions might your novel include?

- Is writing to market something you're interested in? Why?

- If your favorite genre has been declared 'dead', what elements could you add, tweak, or subvert to make it feel fresh?

2.6 What are you writing? Short story, novella, or novel

- Do you know the length of the story you want to write?

- Go back to your list of comparison books. How long are they? What is the reader expectation in the genre?

2.7 What are you writing? Stand-alone, series, or serial

- What kind of stories do you read? Revisit your favorite books and also those that are like what you're writing. Are they stand-alone, series, or serial?

- What kind of story are you writing? How would it be different as a stand-alone, a series, or a serial. Why are you choosing one format over another? (And if you don't know yet, don't worry, you can figure it out along the way).

3.1 Story structure

- Which story structure/s might work best for your idea?

- Which story structures do you want to learn

more about? How will you prevent yourself from drowning in analysis?

- How will you use structure while also bringing originality to your writing?

3.2 Scenes and chapters

- How long is a typical scene in your genre? How long is a chapter? Check your example books and see what the authors do, but don't let them constrain you.

- How long do you expect your chapters and scenes to be?

- Are there a few scenes in your novel you can already clearly visualize? Could writing these scenes first, even if they are out of order, help you get started?

- What are some natural places in your story where you could create cliff-hangers using scene and chapter breaks? Find examples from your favorite books.

- What kind of pacing is typical in your genre? Which techniques for controlling pacing will work well for your novel?

3.3 Character: Who is the story about?

- Make a list of characters from books, movies or TV shows you love. What makes them memorable, interesting, or compelling?

- Who are the different characters in your story? If you know them already, then you can start to make notes about them. If you don't know yet, don't worry, you can create them along the way.

- Why will readers want to spend time with these characters?

- How can you use specific character description and tags to bring them alive? Add these details to your character notes if you have a list already.

- What flaws and wounds might your characters have that add depth and potential to your story? Have you made sure your characters are fully realized, and not purely defined by one thing?

- What are the primary emotions your protagonist will experience over the course of the novel? How can you deepen those emotions and show them on the page?

- What does 'show, don't tell' mean in practice for your novel? For your story, which aspects are most important to show?
- What resources will you use to choose character names?
- How could you use character archetypes to enrich your characters?
- What does your protagonist want? Why do they want it? Can you go deeper into their motivations?
- Who or what is trying to stop your character from getting what they want? What is the antagonist's believable motivation?
- What part does back story play in your story? How much do readers need to know, and how can you weave it into the novel rather than delivering it as an info dump?
- Does your character have an arc in the novel? How do they grow and change?
- How will you integrate aspects of people you know into characters?
- Does your novel include diverse characters? If not, how can you revise your cast of characters

to make it more diverse? What resources will you draw on to make sure your representations are accurate and believable?

3.4 Point of view

- Think about the story you want to tell. How might it change if you choose to write from the perspective of different characters?

- Revisit the five to ten books that are like the story you're writing, or just any of your favorite novels. What POV are they written in? Does it vary by scene or chapter?

- What POV will you write in? What tense will you write in? If you can't decide, just start writing and your preference will probably emerge.

3.5 Dialogue

- In what way do you want to use dialect and speech mannerisms in your story? Why are you making this choice?

- Will you use curse words in your dialogue?

- Select a dialogue-heavy scene from your manuscript and check it against the potential problems listed in this chapter. Which do you need to watch out for, and how can you fix them?

- Similarly, are there tools like subtext or action tags that you could be using more effectively? Are you using dialogue to move the plot forward and/or reveal character?

3.6 Plot: What happens in the story?

- If you aren't already brimming with plot ideas, how might you come up with them?
- What is your main plot?
- What are your subplots?
- How can you raise the stakes so the plot is more engaging to the reader?
- How can you incorporate try/fail cycles into your plot?
- Do the books you enjoy incorporate twists and surprises? How could you work a plot twist into your novel?
- Consider what you expect as a reader in the books you love the most. How can you incorporate such obligatory scenes with an original spin?

- What are some tropes that you love in books, film, and TV? How can you incorporate tropes to satisfy readers while still making them fresh?

- What are some of the story elements that are catnip to you as a reader and as an author? What aspects go on your Id List?

- Do your favorite books use flashbacks? When might they be effective in your novel? Are there other ways of presenting the same story elements?

- Read one of the books you love and note the open questions and open loops that pull you through the story. How can you do the same with your plot?

- Which elements of your plot or characters could you foreshadow early in your story?

- What questions can you ask yourself or your novel if you lose the plot?

3.7 Conflict

- Can you identify the different types of conflict in the books you love or the books that are like what you're writing?

- What would make the situation worse for your characters in each of the categories? How could you layer or amplify the conflict further?

3.8 Openings and endings

- Examine the openings of the books you love. What makes them effective in keeping the reader turning the pages?

- What are some different openings for your book? Think of at least three options. Could the story open later in the plot? What would be the impact of opening in a different place?

- What endings do you remember as being 'just right'? What can you learn from those ending?

- What endings jarred you as a reader? Why did you feel that way?

- Do you already know how your story will end? How can you make that ending as effective as possible?

3.9 Setting and world-building: Where does the story happen?

- What do you know so far about the settings or world of your novel? What do you still need to find out?

- Are you excited about world-building *before* you write? Or is it something you want to discover in the writing process?

- Which of the various aspects of the world will be important for the plot, character development, and/or theme of your novel?

- Have you written specific and sensory detail about each setting to bring it to life? Or do you have talking heads in an empty white room?

- How have you used character emotion to underscore elements of your setting?

- Do you need (or want) to create a world bible? How might it help you?

- How will you balance world-building with writing the novel? How will you stop yourself from drowning in world-building if you find the process enjoyable?

3.10 Author voice

- Pick two established authors in your preferred genre with a number of novels under their belts. Compare the first five chapters of their latest books. Can you pick out elements of their author voice?

- Do you have a sense of your author voice yet? Don't worry if you don't. It will emerge over time.

3.11 Theme

- Do you know the theme you want to write about already? Don't worry if you don't. You can figure it out later.

- Think about the books you love. What are their themes?

- How can you evoke theme in your novel without lecturing the reader?

- How can you deepen your theme?

3.12 Book or story title

- Examine the books on your shelf or your device, especially those by authors you don't buy from based on name recognition. What are some of the common words used in titles? Is there a theme or resonance across them? Write down a list of those words and weigh them up against your story.

- Have a look at the top 100 books in your genre. Write down the titles and see if you can find commonalities.

- What are some other ways you can come up with book titles?

3.13 Language versus story and tools versus art

- Would you rather sell millions of books to millions of happy readers who love your stories? Or would you rather win a literary prize and (most likely) sell fewer copies?

- What do you think is a 'good' book? What do you think is a 'quality' book? Examine your bookshelves for what you buy and read, rather than an intellectual response.

4.1 Attitude to the first draft

- How will you approach the first draft? What attitude shift might help?

4.2 How to write the first draft

- Have you scheduled time blocks for writing in your calendar, not just in your head? Have you actually written them down?
- Have you found a location where you can write without being disturbed?
- Have you found ways to stop yourself from being distracted when you write?
- Are you going to use timed writing sessions? How will you break these up?
- How will you track your progress through the book?
- How will you know when the first draft is finished?
- Do you suffer from shiny object syndrome? Do you have lots of unfinished projects on the go? How will you structure your time so you finish this book? How will you keep yourself focused and on track?

- How much do you want this? What will you say to yourself if you struggle with writing?

4.3 Dictate your book

- Why might you consider dictation? How might it help your writing?
- What's stopping you from dictating? How can you work through those issues in order to try it?
- What method of dictation might work for you?
- What tools do you need to get started?

4.4 Write fast, cycle through, or write slow

- Which of these methods suits you the best? Have you tried other options?

4.5 Writer's block

- If you're struggling with your writing, can you identify the reason behind the block?
- How can you deal with the block and still achieve your goal of writing a book? What practical steps will you take to move your project forward and still look after yourself?

4.6 Writing tools and software

- What tools do you use for writing? What are the pros and cons of them?

- What other tools might be worth trying and why?

4.7 When is the first draft finished?

- What is a finished first draft? How will you know when you have achieved it?

- How will you celebrate the significant milestone of a finished first draft?

- How will you make sure that you are not still writing this novel on your deathbed? Have you set a deadline and worked out your writing schedule?

5.1 Overview of the editing process

- What types of editing might you consider for your manuscript?

5.2 Self-editing

- Have you set aside time for your self-editing process? Have you printed out the manuscript or created a new version with a different font so it looks different to the original?

- Have you shifted your mindset from writer to editor? Do you know what you want the reader's experience to be? How will you keep them in mind as you edit?

- How does your self-editing process work? What tools can you use?

- Is the reader's journey through the book as clear and easy as possible?

- Have you achieved your creative goal for the story? (Or at least made it as far as you can at this point?)

- How will you know when the self-edit is finished? How can you balance doing the best you can with avoiding perfectionism?

- Have you taken this self-editing process as far as you can? Are you ready to work with a professional editor?

5.3 How to find and work with a professional editor

- How will you find a professional editor and validate that they are the right one for you?

- How will you work with your editor so you are both happy with the process and the result?

- How can you prepare yourself mentally for receiving feedback and line edits? How can you reframe the experience as positive and learn for next time?

5.4 Beta readers, specialist readers, and sensitivity readers

- What kind of readers might be useful for your manuscript?

- Where will you find these readers?

- How do you hope to improve the manuscript from this feedback?

- How will you assess whether to make the changes?

5.5 Editing tools and software

- How could you use software to improve your editing process?

5.6 Lessons learned from editing my first novel after more than a decade

- Why are you considering a rewrite? What benefits do you expect to gain from the process? What will make it worth it for you?

- How long has it been since the original release? Is this long enough to make a rewrite worthwhile?

- If you're editing for the first time, what aspects might you need to look out for in your manuscript?

5.7 When is the book finished?

- Have you followed an editorial process to make your book the best it can be within a specific time limit?

- If you're still struggling with the pursuit of perfection, what can you do to move past that?

Acknowledgments

Thank you to my community and patrons at The Creative Penn website and podcast. Your support helps me continue to create after more than a decade of being an independent author.

Thank you to Kristen Tate at The Blue Garret for brilliant editing and advice.

Thanks as ever to Jane Dixon Smith, JD Smith Design, for the cover design and print interior formatting.

www.ingramcontent.com/pod-product-compliance
Lightning Source LLC
Chambersburg PA
CBHW071724080526
44588CB00013B/1884